The Four Seasons of Wolf Trap

A Cookbook to Benefit the
Wolf Trap Foundation for the Performing Arts'
Education Programs

A project of the Wolf Trap Associates

Dedicated to the thousands of Wolf Trap Associates members and volunteers who help Wolf Trap achieve its mission to present and create excellent and innovative performing arts programs for the enrichment, education, and enjoyment of diverse audiences and participants.

© 2005 by the Wolf Trap Foundation for the Performing Arts
1645 Trap Road
Vienna, VA 22182
www.wolftrap.org

ISBN 0-9764964-0-2

First Printing May 2005

Printed in China through Asia Pacific Offset, Inc.
Design by Libby Rector

Color Photographs by Gladys Guzman, Andi Kling, Carol Pratt, and Scott Suchman; Carrier, FoodCollection, Neunsinger, Silverman, and Wieder.

Contents

Wolf Trap
A Gift to America from Catherine Filene Shouse

On summer nights at Wolf Trap, the park is filled with thousands of people enjoying a performance with baskets full of delicious food and drinks. Wolf Trap has always been known as a perfect picnic spot, but did you know that the summer tradition of great food and entertainment started with Wolf Trap's founder Catherine Filene Shouse?

In 1930, Shouse purchased a large farm in Vienna, Virginia, just outside of Washington D.C., that would later become Wolf Trap National Park for the Performing Arts. Although she knew nothing about farming before purchasing the land, she learned to grow her own crops and to raise chickens, hogs, milk cows, and angus steer.

Wolf Trap's Founder, Catherine Filene Shouse

Shouse generously shared her love of the farm with family and friends. She enjoyed cooking gourmet meals and entertaining guests. Over the years, she happily hosted parties, dinners, carnivals, and dances at her farm. The farm earned the reputation of being an excellent, lively gathering place, and invitations to the farm were eagerly sought. Members of the Cabinet, Senate, and House of Representatives, as well as celebrities of the social and arts scenes, were among Shouse's prestigious guests.

Summer Nights Under the Stars

Wolf Trap was a cherished piece of land for Shouse, and she wanted people to enjoy it as much as she. "So many people had grown to love the farm," Shouse said. "That had a good deal to do with my decision to want Wolf Trap to remain permanently for people." In 1964, Shouse offered her property to the federal government to establish the first and only National Park for the Performing Arts. Her offer came at a time when the National Park Service was expanding and interest in the arts in Washington D.C. was growing. In addition to the land, Shouse offered $1,750,000 to build the original outdoor cedar amphitheater for performances.

Throughout the summer, Washingtonians enjoy concerts and picnics in the majestic setting of Wolf Trap National Park for the Performing Arts.

Groundbreaking for the Filene Center began in May 1968, and the first performance was held on July 1, 1971. That year, a unique partnership was forged between the National Park Service, which acts as a steward of the park land and buildings, and Wolf Trap Foundation for the Performing Arts, which provides the programming and administrative support for the performance season. To this day, Wolf Trap remains America's only National Park for the Performing Arts.

Year-Round Performances

In addition to a summer concert space, Shouse envisioned establishing a performing arts venue that brought arts lovers to Wolf Trap year-round. She donated an additional 26 acres of land to the Wolf Trap Foundation for this purpose. In 1981, two 18th century barns were found in upstate New York and reconstructed at Wolf Trap to establish our second performing arts venue, The Barns at Wolf Trap. Shouse felt that the excellent acoustical qualities of these historic barns would provide an ideal

Legendary artists and up-and-coming musicians come to the acoustically-rich Barns at Wolf Trap.

place to experience intimate live performances. The Barns at Wolf Trap continues to showcase worldclass artists from diverse styles and genres of music.

Master teaching artists conduct classroom residencies through the Wolf Trap Institute for Early Learning Through the Arts.

The Arts are at the Center of Learning

Each year over 500,000 people visit the Filene Center and The Barns from all over the country, but Wolf Trap is more than just a great place to see live music. Shouse set forth several goals in her mission for Wolf Trap, which have come to be known as our four pillars. In addition to the Filene Center and The Barns, education and encouraging young talent were very important to Shouse.

From its beginning, Wolf Trap was designed as an educational organization as well as a performing arts venue. Central to the ideology of our most prominent education program, the Wolf Trap Institute for Early Learning Through the Arts, is the use of the arts to help children learn. Since its inception in 1981, the Institute has reached over two million children and adults locally, across the country, and overseas. In 2003, the Center for Education at Wolf Trap was built to allow for the expansion of our nationwide education programs. Built almost exclusively from funds raised from private contributions, the Center for Education serves as the hub for these programs.

Completion of this building signaled a new era for Wolf Trap and furthered its commitment to education.

The Center for Education at Wolf Trap

The Next Generation of Opera Stars

The Center for Education also provides rehearsal space for the world renowned Wolf Trap Opera Company. Established in 1971 to train and showcase promising young vocalists, the Company has helped launch the careers of hundreds of opera singers. The singers, known as Filene Young Artists, are chosen each year from auditions held throughout the country. The selected singers gain invaluable experience performing at both The Barns at Wolf Trap and the Filene Center throughout the summer. The Wolf Trap Opera Company focuses on presenting fully-staged performances in original language.

The Filene Young Artists of the Wolf Trap Opera Company sing the lead roles in both classic and rarely-performed operas.

A Dedicated Core of Supporters and Volunteers

The Wolf Trap Associates program was organized in 1971 for members of the community who want to take an active part in Wolf Trap's mission. The Associates' role in supporting Wolf Trap's education programs cannot be overstated. Associates members and volunteers have a great impact on the work of the Wolf Trap Foundation. Since 1971, the Associates have raised vital financial support for Wolf Trap through special events and fundraisers, as well as through their own annual membership support. Volunteers chair the annual Wolf Trap Ball, the Wolf Trap Gala, the Art for the Arts Show and Sale, and the Golf Tournament and Auction for Education. All of the proceeds from these events support Wolf Trap's education programs. Members also staff the Associates Gift Shop at the Filene Center, and volunteer physicians serve as house doctors at Filene Center performances.

Wolf Trap is a much richer place for the community support it receives from the Associates. The idea for this cookbook and much of the work that has gone into its production came from Wolf Trap Associates members.

—Emily Lu

Wolf Trap Associates and spirited Washingtonians gather on the Filene Center stage each year for the festive Wolf Trap Ball.

7

The Four Seasons of Wolf Trap

Committee

Jean AbiNader, *Co-Chair*
Eloise Poretz, *Co-Chair*

Ted Davis, *Production Director*
Robin Crawford Heller
Ricki Kanter
Lisa LaCamara
Sue Leonard

Creative Team

Frances Bevington
Emily Lu
Libby Rector

Special Thanks

Reico Kitchen and Bath
Alice Duvall
Crystal Diggs
Ellen Fishbein
Virginia Friend
Robin Crawford Heller
Elizabeth Hopkins
Polly Jones
Susan Kadar
Ricki Kanter
Monica Malouf
Kate McConnell
Kristine Moody
Maxine Rapoport
Dana Severson
Margie Wheedleton
Wolf Trap Artists who generously contributed recipes
Wolf Trap Foundation Staff
Wolf Trap National Park for the Performing Arts Staff

Gingery Carrot Soup

It's easy to make, elegant, and comforting too.

1 pound of carrots
1 large onion
3 tablespoons butter
2 1/2 cups chicken broth
1 heaping tablespoon minced fresh ginger
1 teaspoon orange zest
1/2 cup fresh orange juice
1/2 teaspoon black pepper
1/2 teaspoon ground nutmeg or coriander
1/2 teaspoon salt (more or less depending on saltiness of chicken broth)
2-3 sprigs cilantro (optional garnish)

Peel and coarsely chop vegetables. Melt butter in medium saucepan. Add vegetables and sauté 15 minutes. Add 1 cup chicken broth, ginger, and orange zest. Cook partially covered about 1/2 hour or until carrots are soft. Purée in blender, using additional 1 1/2 cups of broth, until perfectly smooth and velvety. Return soup to saucepan. Add orange juice, pepper, and nutmeg or coriander. Taste soup and add salt as needed.

Heat through and serve with whole or chopped fresh cilantro leaves as garnish.

Use extra broth to thin soup (if necessary) if served the next day. Recipe is easy to double. Soup freezes well.

Number of Servings: 4

About the Wolf Trap Opera Company:

Wolf Trap Opera Company was one of the first programs in the country to offer training for young singers.

Spicy Salsa

A spicy salsa that can be served with tortilla chips or crackers.

1 (32 ounce) jar medium
  or hot picante sauce
2 (16 ounce) cans black-
  eyed peas, drained
1 (16 ounce) can white
  hominy, drained
1 cup green bell pepper,
  diced
1 cup white onion,
  chopped
3 large fresh tomatoes,
  chopped
1/2 cup fresh cilantro,
  finely chopped
1/4 cup jalapeño pepper,
  seeded and chopped
1 cup green onions,
  chopped (include
  green tops)
1 tablespoon sugar
1 tablespoon salt
2 tablespoons coarsely
  ground black pepper
2 tablespoons ground
  cumin

Combine first nine ingredients in a very large bowl. Mix together the next four ingredients, then combine with first mixture. Serve with tortilla chips.

Number of Servings: 8-10

Cool-as-a-Cucumber Soup

This is an easy recipe that can be made ahead. It's a wonderful starter for an evening picnic at the Filene Center.

3 large cucumbers, peeled and seeded
Coarse salt
1 can low fat cream of celery soup
3 green onions, sliced
2-3 cups nonfat chicken broth (vegetable broth may be substituted for a fully vegetarian recipe)
1 tablespoon fresh dill (or 1½ tablespoons dried dill)
1 (16 ounce) container nonfat plain yogurt (reserve ⅓ cup)
Fresh dill sprigs

Slice peeled and seeded cucumbers into ½ inch slices. Place in colander and toss with coarse salt. Allow to drain for 30 minutes (this reduces bitterness). Rinse well with cold water. Place cucumber slices into blender. Add cream of celery soup, green onions, and 2 cups of the chicken broth. Blend slowly, gradually increasing speed to purée mixture. Add dill and blend again. Pour blended mixture into large bowl. Whisk in nonfat yogurt.

If mixture is too thick, add rest of chicken broth to desired consistency. Chill thoroughly, preferably overnight. Serve in bowl with a dollop of reserved yogurt and sprig of fresh dill.

Number of Servings: 4 generously or can be stretched to 8 when served in small bowls or cups as an appetizer.

About the Wolf Trap Opera Company:

The company's productions of *The Magic Flute* in 1985 and *The Love of Three Oranges* in 1988 featured sets and costumes designed by Maurice Sendak, author of the children's book *Where the Wild Things Are*.

Diva Mamma Mo's Hummus

Maureen McGovern - Cabaret Performer

As they say, 'busy women never cook!' Therefore, I don't cook, I combine. Enjoy!

8 ounces prepared Kalamata olive hummus

8 ounces prepared roasted garlic hummus

8 ounces prepared roasted red pepper hummus

8 ounces prepared 40 spices hummus

2-3 tablespoons black olive tapenade

Simply combine first four ingredients, add olive tapenade, sprinkle, and serve! Couldn't be easier, tastes great, and your guests won't believe it was that easy!

Serve with pita bread (lightly toasted), Mediterranean veggie chips, rye crisps, favorite crackers, or vegetable crudités.

Number of Servings: 8-10

Bourbon Sausage

Delicious and very easy to prepare.

1 1/2 pounds mild pork sausage

1 1/2 pounds hot smoked sausage

1 cup bourbon

1 cup brown sugar, firmly packed

1 cup chili sauce

Slice sausage into 1/2-1 inch pieces. Place in large casserole dish. Combine bourbon, brown sugar, and chili sauce and pour the mix over the sausage. Bake, covered, 2-2 1/2 hours at 350 degrees. Serve with toothpicks. Keep warm in a chafing dish.

Number of Servings: about 20

About the Wolf Trap Opera Company:

The singers of the Opera Company are in residence at Wolf Trap each summer for 10-12 weeks, performing in three operas as well as recital and concert presentations.

Black Bean Dip

A refreshing tasty corn and tomato black bean dip that can be eaten in a pita pocket or with your favorite corn chips.

1 (15 ounce) can black beans, drained and rinsed
1 small can whole kernel corn
2 medium tomatoes, diced
1 green pepper, diced
1 red bell pepper, diced
$1/2$ cup red onion, diced
$1/3$ cup lime juice
$1/4$ cup olive oil
1 jalapeño pepper, seeded and diced
1 teaspoon salt (optional)
$1/3$ cup parsley, chopped
$1/2$ teaspoon cumin
$1/2$ teaspoon chili powder

Combine all ingredients in a large bowl. Mix well and serve with corn chips.

Number of Servings: 6-8

"Plains Special" Cheese Ring

Former First Lady, Mrs. Rosalynn Carter

This recipe has been a favorite of the Carter family and the community of Plains for many years. It was also served when the Carters lived in the Georgia Governor's Mansion and was a popular dish in the White House, too.

1 pound sharp cheese, grated
1 cup mixed nuts, finely chopped
1 cup mayonnaise
1 small onion, finely grated
   Ground black pepper to taste
   Dash cayenne pepper
   Strawberry preserves (optional)

Combine all ingredients except preserves in a small mixing bowl. Season to taste with pepper. Mix and place in a 5 or 6 cup lightly greased ring mold. Refrigerate until firm for several hours or overnight.

To serve, unmold, and if desired, fill center with strawberry preserves, or serve plain with crackers.

Number of Servings: 8-10

Chunky Gazpacho

Featured in the Wolf Trap Picnic cookbook published in 1976, this is a favorite summer recipe.

6 large ripe tomatoes, peeled, seeded, and chopped

2 cucumbers, peeled, seeded, and chopped

1 clove garlic, finely minced

$1/2$ cup green or red pepper, seeded and chopped

$1/2$ cup onion, peeled and finely chopped

$2^{1}/2$ cups tomato juice (or cocktail vegetable juice)

$1/4$ cup and 1 tablespoon olive oil

3 tablespoons lemon juice
Hot sauce, salt, and pepper to taste

Garnish:

6 parsley sprigs
Garlic croutons

Combine chopped raw vegetables in a large serving bowl. Mix together the tomato juice, olive oil, and lemon juice. Pour over vegetables and mix. Add salt, pepper, and hot sauce to taste. Chill. To serve, pour the soup over an ice cube in each cup or bowl. Garnish with a sprig of parsley and garlic croutons.

Number of Servings: 6

Holiday Season Deviled Eggs

A stunning addition to your holiday buffet.

12-18 hard-boiled eggs, cooled with shells removed and halved lengthwise

Ham relish:
$\frac{1}{2}$ egg yolks from hard-boiled eggs
1 (6 ounce) can deviled ham
$1\frac{1}{2}$ tablespoons pickle relish (sweet or dill)
$\frac{1}{2}$ teaspoon dry mustard
Salt and pepper to taste
2 tablespoons mayonnaise

Tuna relish:
$\frac{1}{2}$ egg yolks from hard-boiled eggs
1 (6 ounce) can drained water-packed tuna
$1\frac{1}{2}$ tablespoons pickle relish
$\frac{1}{2}$ teaspoon curry powder
Salt and pepper to taste
2 tablespoons mayonnaise

Prepare ham and tuna relish. Fill half the whites of eggs with the ham relish, and dust liberally with paprika.

Fill half the whites of eggs with the tuna relish, and dust liberally with chopped fresh chives (or basil or parsley).

Arrange on a serving platter, alternating red and green eggs.

Number of Servings: 24-36

Couscous Salad

A perfect summer dish. Great with chicken or beef off the grill.

1 (6 ounce) box couscous
1 (6 ounce) can artichoke
  hearts, quartered and
  diced
$1/4$ cup red bell pepper,
  diced
$1^1/2$ tablespoons lemon
  juice
2 grilled carrots, cut on
  bias
1 cup diced mozzarella
  cheese (optional)
$1/2$ cup toasted walnut
  pieces
$1^1/2$ tablespoons dill
  Salt and pepper to taste
$1/4$ cup chopped fresh basil
3 tablespoons olive oil

Prepare couscous according to package. Fluff and cool completely.

Toss with remaining ingredients and allow to marinate 2 or more hours in refrigerator.

Number of Servings: 6-8

Quick and Easy Artichoke Dip

A tasty, inexpensive appetizer that people will ask for time and again.

1 (14 ounce) can
   artichokes, drained
   and chopped
1 cup mayonnaise
1 cup Parmesan cheese,
   grated
$\frac{1}{2}$ teaspoon garlic salt
   Dash of lemon juice

Lightly grease casserole dish and preheat oven to 350 degrees.

Mix ingredients in medium size bowl with wooden spoon. Pour into lightly greased casserole dish and bake at 350 degrees for $\frac{1}{2}$ hour or until top is brown and inside is not runny. Serve with crackers or French bread.

Number of Servings: 8-10

About the Wolf Trap Opera Company:

Each foreign language opera that Wolf Trap produces employs a diction coach who works with the Opera Company singers in that language. Performing operas in their original languages gives the young singers invaluable experience.

Chunky Chicken Salad

Rebecca Lynn Howard - Country Music Performer

This salad is one of my very favorite things to eat. You can enjoy this on celery, crackers, bread, or my personal choice, in tomatoes!

3 large boneless, skinless chicken breasts
$1/2$ cup seedless red or green grapes, cut in half
$1/2$ cup pecans, whole or chopped
$1/2$ cup mandarin orange slices
2 celery stalks, chopped
2 tablespoons sour cream
$1/2$ cup light mayonnaise
Salt and pepper to taste

Heat oven to 375 degrees. Place chicken in glass pan. Fill pan with water until chicken is almost submerged. Place pan in oven and let cook for 2 hours. This will make it extra tender. After cooking, shred chicken by hand, using a fork, until finely shredded. Place in a large mixing bowl.

Cut grapes in half and add the "chunky" ingredients. Pecans can be added whole or chopped. Mandarin orange slices can be added whole. Mix ingredients then add wet ingredients. Stir until chunky ingredients are covered by the sour cream and the light mayonnaise. Finally add salt and pepper to taste. Refrigerate until chilled and enjoy!

Number of Servings: 6

About the Wolf Trap Opera Company:

The Company's 1974-1976 productions of *The Daughter of the Regiment*, *Roberto Devereux*, and *La traviata*, all starring Beverly Sills, were recorded for television and aired nationally.

Sweet Potato Soup with Coconut and Ginger

This recipe combines flavors of the Pacific and the Deep South to produce a soup that warms your tummy.

2 large onions, diced
2 ounces butter
8 ounces fresh ginger, peeled and sliced into thin coins
3 cups coconut milk*
3½ pounds sweet potatoes, peeled and diced
2 quarts chicken stock
1 tablespoon cider vinegar
Salt and white pepper to taste

*Thai coconut milk is very creamy and rich and adds to the texture of the finished soup.

Dice the onions and cook them slowly in butter until they are tender. While the onions are cooking, slice the ginger into thin coins. Place them in a pot with the coconut milk, bring to a boil and simmer gently for about 45 minutes. Set the coconut milk and ginger aside. When the onions are tender, add the diced sweet potatoes and chicken stock. Bring to a boil and simmer until the potatoes are completely soft.

When the potatoes are ready, strain the coconut milk and discard the ginger. Add the infused coconut milk and cider vinegar to the soup. Purée mixture in food processor until the soup is very smooth.

Season to taste with salt and white pepper.

Number of Servings: 6-8

Chili Dip

A rich, thick salsa-type dip.

1 (14.5 ounce) can
   pitted black olives
1 (14.5 ounce) can
   stewed or diced tomato
1 small can sliced green
   jalapeño peppers
1 small onion,
   finely chopped
$1/8$ cup vinegar
$1/8$ cup olive oil
   Dash of Worcestershire
   sauce
   Garlic salt and pepper to
   taste

Rinse, drain, and finely chop the olives. Mix all the ingredients together. Refrigerate for at least two hours to let the flavors blend. Serve with tortilla chips.

Note:
You can use a food processor to combine the ingredients, but be careful to pulse briefly, so as not to make "soup."

Number of Servings: 8-12

Lime Soup with Chilies and Tortillas

This is a common dish on the Yucatan Peninsula of Mexico. Very refreshing, even in hot weather! A terrific starter before quesadillas or fajitas.

2 cups cooked and shredded chicken breasts (2-3 breasts)
1 cup olive oil
3 (6-inch) corn tortillas, cut into ¹/₂ inch strips
1 tablespoon vegetable oil
1 cup chopped onion
2 cloves garlic, finely chopped
8 cups chicken broth (low salt) or 4 cups broth and 4 cups stock
1 (14.5 ounce) can peeled and diced tomatoes, drained
1 (4 ounce) can diced green chilies
¹/₂ cup lime juice (3-4 limes)
¹/₂ teaspoon cumin
¹/₄ teaspoon ground pepper
1 lime sliced into 6 slices
3 tablespoons fresh cilantro, chopped (optional)

Boil chicken breasts about 25 minutes or until done (not pink inside) let cool and finely shred chicken breasts with fork.

Heat 1 cup olive oil in medium skillet over medium heat. Working in batches, add tortilla strips to oil; fry until golden (about 2 minutes) transfer to paper towels to drain. Heat vegetable oil in large saucepan over medium heat. Sauté onion and garlic for 3-4 minutes or until onion is tender. Add broth, tomatoes, chilies, lime juice, cumin, and pepper, bring to boil. Reduce heat to low, simmer uncovered for 8-10 minutes. Add chicken; simmer for another 3-4 minutes.

Place 1 lime slice in each of 6 bowls. Ladle hot soup over lime. Mound tortilla strips in center of bowl and sprinkle with cilantro to garnish just before serving.

Tortilla strips and soup can be made one day ahead. Store strips in airtight container at room temperature.

Number of Servings: 6

Rice Salad with Capers, Pine Nuts, Chives, and Oregano

An excellent summer salad that can be made ahead of time. Enjoy with beef, chicken, or fish.

Dressing:
- 2 tablespoons fresh lemon juice
- 2 tablespoons sherry vinegar
- 1 tablespoon shallot, minced
- $3/4$ teaspoon salt
- 4 dashes hot sauce
- $1/2$ cup olive oil

Rice:
- 4 cups water
- 2 cups white rice
- $1 1/2$ teaspoons salt
- 2 bay leaves
- 2 tablespoons fresh or dried oregano
- $1/2$ cup toasted pine nuts
- $1/2$ cup drained capers
- 2 tablespoons chopped fresh or dried chives

Whisk together first 5 ingredients in dressing. Gradually whisk in oil. (Can be made 1 day in advance. Cover and chill.)

Cook rice with salt and bay leaves. Remove bay leaves and place rice in medium size bowl. Add dressing and oregano. Cover and refrigerate.

Mix pine nuts, capers, and chives into rice. Let stand for 10-15 minutes for flavors to be absorbed, and serve.

Number of Servings: 6-8

Guacamole

Paul Taylor - Choreographer

Just the thing to enjoy during a blizzard while pretending to be in the tropics. Good with tortilla chips and especially rum and Coca-Cola.

2 ripe avocados
1 tablespoon onion juice
1 tablespoon lemon juice
   (or lime)
   Salt to taste
1 ripe tomato, minced
1 scallion, minced
$1/2$ teaspoon chili powder
1 teaspoon olive oil
$1/2$ teaspoon coriander

Peel avocado. Mash pulp with a fork. Add ingredients just before serving. Mix well. Garnish with paprika and parsley if you want to get fancy.

Number of Servings: 4-8

About the Wolf Trap Opera Company:

Important American works presented by the Opera Company include Gian-Carlo Menotti's *The Saint of Bleecker Street*, Douglas Ward's *The Crucible*, Conrad Susa's *Transformations*, Marc Blitzstein's *Regina*, and Dominick Argento's *Postcard from Morocco*.

Tortellini Soup with Kielbasa and Kale

2 tablespoons olive oil
12 ounces smoked kielbasa sausage, fully cooked and thinly sliced
1 onion, chopped
1 cup fennel bulb, cored and chopped
4 cloves garlic, minced
1$\frac{1}{2}$ tablespoons fresh thyme, chopped
$\frac{1}{2}$ teaspoon dried red pepper flakes
10 cups low-salt chicken broth
1 (15 ounce) can cannellini beans, rinsed with warm water and drained
1 (9 ounce) package cheese tortellini
4 cups fresh kale, spines discarded and leaves chopped
   Parmesan or asiago cheese, grated

Heat the oil in a large pot over medium-high heat. Add the next 6 ingredients and sauté until the vegetables are soft and the kielbasa is brown, about 12 minutes. Add the broth and bring to a boil. Stir in the cannellini beans; reduce the heat to low and simmer for 4 minutes. (Can be made one day ahead, cool slightly, cover and chill. Bring to a simmer before continuing.)

Add the tortellini to the soup, cook for 1 minute and then add the kale and cook for 4 minutes more.

To serve:
Ladle into bowls and sprinkle with cheese.

Note:
This is a very spicy soup; cut down on the red pepper flakes if you want it milder.

Number of Servings: 6

Endive with Caviar

Easy and delicious.

¾ cup (6 ounces) fat free
   cream cheese, softened
1¼ teaspoons fresh chives,
   chopped (or 1 teaspoon
   dried chives)
1¼ teaspoons pecans,
   finely chopped
1¼ teaspoons fat free
   mayonnaise
2 medium heads Belgian
   endive, separated into
   individual leaves
4 tablespoons red caviar

Combine first four ingredients in medium size mixing bowl; beat at medium speed with an electric mixer until smooth. Spread mixture into the middle of endive leaves and lightly sprinkle red caviar on top.

Presentation:
Use a round dark colored platter and fan the endive leaves from center outward. In the center place a small bowl and remaining caviar with a small, attractive serving spoon.

Number of Servings: 8

About the Wolf Trap Opera Company:

In 1998, world-renowned opera singer and Wolf Trap Opera alumna Denyce Graves headlined the Wolf Trap Gala with Leonard Slatkin and the National Symphony Orchestra. One of Washington, D.C.'s premier fundraising events, the Gala gives guests the opportunity to mingle with members of the Washington social scene and often the Gala performers themselves.

Sour Cream Chicken Mousse

A great spring appetizer.

2 envelopes unflavored gelatin
2 cups boiling water (or 2 cups chicken broth)
4 chicken bouillon cubes
3 tablespoons lemon juice
1 teaspoon dry mustard
2½ teaspoons curry powder
1 teaspoon onion salt
2 cups sour cream
3 cups chicken, cooked and diced
1 cup celery, chopped
¼ cup green pepper, chopped
¼ cup roasted almonds, diced

Garnish:
Fresh watercress sprigs
Crackers

In large bowl, sprinkle gelatin over surface of ½ cup cold water; let stand about 5 minutes. Pour boiling water over bouillon cubes, add lemon juice, mustard, curry powder, and onion salt. (Chicken stock can be substituted for water and bouillon cubes.) Let cool about 5 minutes.

Mix with gelatin and stir in sour cream, mixing well. Refrigerate until consistency of unbeaten egg white, about 40 minutes. Fold chicken, celery, green pepper, and almonds into gelatin mixture. Mix well.

Turn into 1½ quart mold or 8 (6 ounce) custard cups. Refrigerate covered until firm, 4 hours minimum for large mold. To unmold, run spatula around edge of mold to loosen, invert over serving platter and shake gently to release.

Serve garnished with watercress sprigs and your favorite crackers or bread.

Number of Servings: 8

Watercress Salad

Brian McBride, Executive Chef

Melrose Restaurant
Park Hyatt Hotel
1201 24th Street, NW
Washington, DC 22037

This favorite salad from Melrose Restaurant accompanies the recipe on page 82.

2 bunches very fresh
  watercress
1½ tablespoons olive oil
1 teaspoon fresh lemon
  juice
  Salt and freshly ground
  pepper to taste

Wash the watercress and trim off the very bottom of the stems. Transfer to a non-reactive bowl and toss with the oil, lemon juice, salt, and pepper.

Number of Servings: 6

About the Wolf Trap Opera Company:

Wolf Trap Opera Company members stay with local "housing hosts" during their summer residencies. Each year about 25 families generously open up their homes to host these young artists. It is a great opportunity to get to know these future opera stars!

Cheese Krispies

Great little bites to include in your cocktail hour.

½ pound margarine
½ pound sharp cheese, grated
2 cups flour
2 teaspoons sugar
1 teaspoon salt
Dash red pepper
2 cups crisp rice cereal
¾ cup pecans, chopped

Mix softened margarine and grated cheese together. Blend in the other ingredients, folding in crisp rice cereal last. Chill 1 hour.

Shape into small balls and press down on a cookie sheet with a fork. Also may be formed into several long small rolls before chilling; slice into ¼ inch slices when firm. Bake at 350 degrees for 15 minutes. Serve hot or at room temperature.

Number of Servings: 20-25

About the Wolf Trap Opera Company:

In 2004, the Company performed Salieri's *Falstaff*, an almost-forgotten work by this well-known contemporary and rival of Mozart. "Each summer, [the Wolf Trap Opera Company] coddles some of the best, most innovative and theatrically experimental opera in the area—in small, loving shows of interesting repertoire presented at the tiny Barns [at] Wolf Trap." —*The Washington Post*

The Ultimate Hot Spinach Dip

The Honorable and Mrs. Newt Gingrich

This dip reaches its fullest potential when served with a glass of Chardonnay!

- 1 package frozen spinach
- 1 stick butter or margarine
- 1 package cream cheese
- 1/2 cup sour cream
- 1/4 cup Parmesan cheese (optional)
  Splash of soy sauce (or hot sauce if you prefer)
- 1 large can artichoke hearts
- 1 can water chestnuts
- 1 cup seasoned bread crumbs

Prepare spinach as directed on package. Mix cooked spinach, 1/2 stick butter, cream cheese, sour cream, Parmesan cheese, and soy sauce in a bowl.

Cut up artichokes and water chestnuts, mix together in another bowl. Spray medium size baking dish with cooking spray. Layer the following: artichoke/water chestnut mixture, spinach mixture, artichoke/water chestnut mixture, spinach mixture. Top with seasoned bread crumbs. Drizzle with 1/2 stick butter or margarine.

Bake for 30 minutes at 325 degrees.

Enjoy with crackers, hard sourdough bread, or tortilla chips.

Number of Servings: 8-10

About the Wolf Trap Opera Company:

In addition to performing full-length operas each summer, the Opera Company members present two multi-singer recitals each season. Steven Blier of the New York Festival of Song joins the Company members for these regularly sold-out performances, such as the humorous and lighthearted "Girls Just Want to Have Fun" in 2004.

Summer Potato Salad

A beautiful and refreshing accompaniment to summertime grilled foods!

4 cups red potatoes with skins, cooked and sliced
1/2 cup cucumber, chopped
1 medium onion, minced
3/4 teaspoon celery seed
1 1/2 teaspoons salt
1/2 teaspoon pepper
3 hard-boiled eggs, sliced
1 1/2 cups sour cream
1/2 cup mayonnaise
1/4 cup white vinegar
1 teaspoon dry mustard
3 radishes, sliced (optional)

Combine potatoes, cucumber, onion, celery seed, salt, pepper, and egg whites in a large bowl.

In another bowl, combine egg yolks, sour cream, mayonnaise, vinegar, and mustard. Add cream mixture to dry ingredients and mix well. Garnish with radishes or mix them in.

Cover and refrigerate. Serve chilled.

Number of Servings: 8

About the Wolf Trap Opera Company:

"The polish and sparkle one expects from a world-class professional company."
—*The Washington Post*

Apricot and Lentil Soup

A unique and hearty soup for fall, this recipe is easy to follow.

1 1/2 cups dried lentils
  6 cups vegetable stock
    or water
  3/4 cup dried apricots,
    chopped
3-4 tablespoons
    vegetable oil
  1 cup onions, chopped
  3 cups eggplant,
    peeled and cubed
1 1/2 cups tomatoes, chopped
    (fresh or canned)
  1 green pepper, chopped
  1/2 teaspoon cinnamon
  1/4 teaspoon cayenne
    pepper
  1 tablespoon paprika
1 1/2 teaspoons salt (optional)
  3 tablespoons fresh parsley,
    chopped (optional)
  1 tablespoon fresh mint,
    chopped (optional)

Rinse lentils and then bring them to a boil in the stock or water. Reduce heat and simmer covered for 20 minutes. Add chopped apricots and simmer covered for another 20 minutes.

In the meantime, sauté onions in oil until translucent. Add eggplant and 4-5 tablespoons of water. Cook covered on medium heat, stirring occasionally until eggplant is almost tender. Add remaining vegetables, dried spices, and salt. Cover and cook until tender, about 10 minutes.

Stir the sautéed vegetables into the cooked lentil apricot mixture and simmer for 15 minutes. Add the parsley and mint. Serve with a delicious cheese, fresh baked bread, and a green salad.

Number of Servings: 6

Goldy's Bodacious Buffalo Wings

Goldy - Radio Personality

I've been perfecting it for three decades…here it is for your enjoyment!

Celery sticks
1 jar prepared blue
   cheese dressing
1/4 cup (1/2 stick) butter
2 1/2 tablespoons hot sauce
   (or more if you dare!)
2 tablespoons red wine
   vinegar
   Oil for deep frying
3 pounds of wings

Prepare celery sticks and blue cheese dressing and chill.

Slowly melt butter in a saucepan. Add the hot sauce and vinegar. Keep warm.

Heat oil in a large frying pan to about 350 degrees. Deep-fry wings until nicely browned and crisp, about 15 minutes. Remove and drain on paper towels.

Give each person their own small bowl of sauce and some wings and let them do their own dipping. Serve with celery sticks and blue cheese on the side. Call and thank me later!

Number of Servings: 8-10

Chopped Salad

Very colorful presentation when served in a glass bowl.

Salad:
- 1 cup hearts of palm, rinsed and diced
- 1 cup cucumber, peeled, seeded, and diced
- 1 cup grape tomatoes, washed, cut in $1/2$ inch dice and drained
- 1 cup (about 6 ounces) feta cheese, crumbled
- $1/2$ cup scallions, washed, trimmed, and diced
- $1/4$ cup toasted pine nuts, (optional)
- 3 tablespoons fresh parsley, chopped

Dressing:
- $1/3$ cup extra virgin olive oil
- 2 tablespoons red wine vinegar
- $1/2$ teaspoon coarse ground pepper
- $1/4$ teaspoon salt (optional)

Salad:
Place all of the salad ingredients in a bowl, cover, and chill until needed.

Dressing:
Combine all of the ingredients in a small bowl. Set aside until needed.

To serve:
Stir up the dressing, pour it over the salad, and toss to mix. Serve immediately.

Number of Servings: 6

Salmon Paté

Smokey and rich.

1 large can red salmon
2 teaspoons onion, grated
8 ounces cream cheese
1 tablespoon lemon juice
2 tablespoons horseradish
$1/4$ teaspoon salt
$1/2$ teaspoon liquid smoke
  Add chopped fresh dill
  to taste (optional)

Drain salmon and take out bones. Mix remaining ingredients together well in a small bowl or food processor.

Wrap in plastic wrap in shape of a roll or put in a small mold. Refrigerate until firm, about two hours.

Serve with rye bread, cucumber slices, or crackers.

Number of Servings: 6-8

About the Wolf Trap Opera Company:

The Wolf Trap Opera Company receives over 500 applications each fall. Approximately 350 are heard in live nationwide auditions, and 12-15 are selected for the Company.

Classic Panzanella

The classic dish with an abundance of fresh flavors.

1 medium red onion
   (about 6 ounces), peeled
   and thinly sliced
5 thick slices of stale
   rustic style bread
1 teaspoon coarse salt
2 pounds ripe beefsteak
   tomatoes, cored and cut
   into large chunks
1 medium bunch green
   onions, chopped
4 cucumbers (about
   12 ounces) peeled and
   sliced
5 tablespoons extra-virgin
   olive oil
3 tablespoons red wine
   vinegar
   Coarse salt and freshly
   ground pepper
1 cup packed fresh basil
   leaves
   Mozzarella, feta, or
   Parmesan cheese
   (optional)

Fill bowl with enough cold water to cover onion slices. Let onion soak about 30 minutes changing the water three or four times. Drain, and transfer to a large bowl or dish. Cover bread with cold water, and let stand until the bread is softened and heavy with water, about 10 minutes.

Squeeze the bread between your palms to remove as much water as possible. Arrange bread on a double layer of paper towels. Cover with another double layer of paper towels, and press down to extract any remaining water. Remove top layer of towels, and sprinkle bread with about 1 teaspoon salt. Set aside for 5 minutes. Using fingers, pluck bread into bite size pieces, and transfer to the dish containing the onions.

Add the tomatoes, green onions, and cucumbers. Drizzle the oil and vinegar over the salad, season with salt and pepper. Tear the basil leaves in half; add to the bowl. Gently toss to combine. Set aside in a cool place for 30-45 minutes. Toss, sprinkle with cheese if desired, and serve.

Number of Servings: 6

Cold Beet Soup

Beautiful and tasty.

4 medium beets, cooked, cooled, peeled, and diced (To cook and peel, cut beet top and bottom, wrap in foil, bake at 350 degrees for 1 hour)
1 cucumber, peeled, seeded, and diced
¼ small white onion, peeled and chopped
1 cup fresh bread crumbs
3 cups lowfat sour cream (or 2 cups buttermilk and 1 cup lowfat sour cream)
2 tablespoons heavy cream, plus more for garnish
2 tablespoons red wine vinegar
1 tablespoon balsamic vinegar
2 tablespoons Dijon mustard
1 tablespoon sugar
Salt and pepper to taste

Combine everything but the salt and pepper into a medium glass, ceramic, or plastic bowl and mix well. Cover and chill overnight. The next day, purée the mixture in a food processor until smooth. Season with salt and pepper to taste.

To serve:
Ladle into bowls and drizzle with heavy cream if desired. Serve chilled.

Number of Servings: 6

Green Bean and Pear Salad with Candied Walnuts

Juicy pears and candied walnuts—the perfect combination of flavors.

For walnuts:
- Nonstick vegetable oil cooking spray
- 1 cup walnuts
- 2 tablespoons sugar
- 1 tablespoon water

For salad:
- 1/3 cup olive oil
- 1/3 cup walnut oil or olive oil
- 3 tablespoons white wine vinegar
- 1 tablespoon fresh parsley, chopped
- 1 tablespoon fresh tarragon, minced
- Salt and pepper
- 1 cup red onion, very thinly sliced
- 12 ounces green beans, ends trimmed
- 2 Bosc pears (about 12 ounces), peeled, quartered, cored, cut into thin strips
- 1 (5 ounce) bag mixed baby greens
- Blue cheese, crumbled (optional)

For walnuts:
Preheat oven to 350 degrees. Spray baking sheet with nonstick spray. Scatter walnuts on prepared sheet. Sprinkle with sugar, then water. Shake baking sheet several times to coat nuts evenly. Bake nuts until golden and coated with sugar, stirring 3 times, about 12 minutes. Cool completely on sheet.

For salad:
Whisk olive oil, walnut oil, vinegar, parsley, and tarragon in medium bowl to blend. Season dressing generously with salt and pepper. Mix in onions. Cook beans in large pot of boiling salted water until just crisp-tender, about 4 minutes. Drain, pat dry, and cool completely.

Using slotted spoon, transfer onions from dressing to large bowl. Add pears and mixed baby greens. Cut beans into 2 inch lengths and add to salad. Toss to blend, adding all or part of remaining dressing as desired. Season with salt and pepper.

To serve:
Divide salad among plates; garnish with candied walnuts. Top with crumbled blue cheese.

Number of Servings: 8

Orzo with Everything

A perfect pasta salad that's loaded with flavorful ingredients.

1½ cups (10 ounces) orzo (rice-shaped pasta)
⅓ cup (packed) oil-packed sun-dried tomatoes, drained and chopped
5 tablespoons extra-virgin olive oil
¼ cup balsamic vinegar
¼ cup (packed) chopped Kalamata olives
1 cup radicchio, finely chopped (about 1 small head)

1 cup arugula, finely chopped
½ cup toasted pine nuts
½ cup fresh basil, chopped
½ cup Parmesan cheese, freshly grated
2 large garlic cloves, minced

Cook orzo in pot of boiling salted water until just tender but still firm to bite. Drain well. Transfer to large bowl. Add sun-dried tomatoes, oil, vinegar, and olives and toss to blend. Let stand until cool. (Can be prepared 6 hours ahead. Cover and refrigerate. Bring to room temperature before continuing.)

Mix chopped radicchio, arugula, pine nuts, chopped basil, Parmesan, and garlic into orzo mixture. Season salad to taste with salt and pepper and serve.

Number of Servings: 6-8

About the Wolf Trap Opera Company:

Wolf Trap commissioned its first opera in 2001 from award-winning composer John Musto. The world premiere of this comic opera, *Volpone* (The Fox), played to sold-out houses for its three-performance run at The Barns at Wolf Trap in March, 2004.

Barley and Corn Salad with Arugula and Green Beans

A delicious hearty salad.

²/3 cup pearl barley
1 pound green beans, trimmed
1 cup fresh corn kernels (1 large ear)
4 large bunches arugula (about 4 ounces total)

¹/2 cup extra-virgin olive oil
¹/4 cup white wine vinegar
3 tablespoons shallots, minced
2 tablespoons fresh thyme, minced
2 teaspoons Dijon mustard
Salt and pepper to taste

1 (3¹/2 ounce) package soft fresh goat cheese, crumbled
1 tablespoon fresh parsley, chopped
Red pear tomatoes, halved (optional)

Cook barley in medium saucepan of boiling salted water until tender, about 30 minutes. Drain; cool. Transfer to large bowl.

Cook beans in large pot of boiling salted water until crisp-tender, about 4 minutes. Drain. Transfer beans to bowl of ice water to cool. Drain well. Pat beans dry with paper towels. Cut half of beans into 2 inch pieces. Transfer to bowl with barley. Mix in corn kernels. Coarsely chop 2 bunches arugula; add to bowl with barley mixture.

Whisk olive oil, vinegar, shallots, thyme, and Dijon mustard in small bowl to blend. Pour enough dressing over barley mixture to coat. Season salad to taste with salt and pepper.

Arrange remaining 2 bunches arugula around edge of large platter. Arrange remaining whole beans in spoke pattern atop arugula. Mound salad in center of platter. Sprinkle with goat cheese. Drizzle any remaining dressing over arugula and beans and serve. Garnish with chopped fresh parsley and pear tomatoes.

Number of Servings: 6

Jicama, Mango, and Watercress Salad

An unusual combination of flavors.

Vinaigrette:
  ¾ cup walnut oil or
    olive oil
  6 tablespoons white
    wine vinegar
  5 tablespoons fresh cilantro
    or parsley, chopped
  3 tablespoons toasted pecans,
    chopped
    Salt and pepper to taste

Salad:
  2 large bunches watercress,
    trimmed
  2 cups jicama, peeled and
    cut into 2 inch long
    matchstick size strips
  2 cups mango, peeled and
    cut into 2 inch long
    matchstick size strips
  2 small red bell peppers,
    cut into 2 inch long
    matchstick size strips
  ½ cup toasted pecan halves

For vinaigrette:
Whisk walnut oil, white wine vinegar, and chopped fresh cilantro in small bowl. Stir in pecans. Season to taste with salt and pepper. (Can be prepared 2 hours ahead.)

For Salad:
Combine watercress, jicama, mango, and red bell peppers in large bowl. Toss with enough dressing to coat. Season with salt and pepper. Divide salad among plates. Sprinkle with pecans and serve.

This salad also works well with arugula.

Number of Servings: 8

Green Vegetable Salad with Orange-Hazelnut Dressing

Lovely flavorful salad perfect for a crowd.

1½ pounds sugar snap peas, stemmed, strings removed

1½ pounds green beans, cut into 1 inch long pieces

2 large broccoli bunches, stemmed, cut into florets

2 pounds asparagus, trimmed, cut into 1 inch long pieces

1 large green pepper, seeded and diced

Dressing:

1½ cup olive oil (preferably extra-virgin)

⅔ cup red wine vinegar

⅔ cup orange juice

2 tablespoons orange peel, grated

¾ cup toasted hazelnuts, finely chopped

Peel (orange part only) from one orange, cut into thin strips

For salad:
Bring large pot of salted water to boil. Add sugar snap peas and cook until bright green and crisp, about 1 minute. Using slotted spoon, transfer peas to bowl of ice water and cool. Drain peas. Return water in pot to boil. Add green beans and cook until crisp-tender, about 5 minutes. Using slotted spoon, transfer beans to bowl of ice water and cool. Drain beans. Return water in pot to boil. Add broccoli and asparagus and cook until crisp-tender, about 3 minutes. Drain well. Transfer to bowl of ice water and cool. Drain broccoli and asparagus thoroughly. Combine all vegetables in large bowl. Cover and chill. (Can be prepared 1 day ahead.)

For dressing:
Whisk first four dressing ingredients in small bowl. Mix in hazelnuts.

Pour dressing over vegetables and toss gently. Garnish with orange peel strips and serve.

Number of Servings: 15

Stuffed Mushrooms à la Colonna

Can be prepared in the morning and baked in the evening.

12 large mushrooms
¼ cup butter, melted
2-3 tablespoons shallots or
   scallions, finely chopped
   Salt and pepper to taste
2 very generous
   tablespoons butter
½ tablespoon flour
½ cup heavy or
   table cream
3 tablespoons fresh parsley,
   chopped
4-5 tablespoons Swiss
   cheese, grated

Remove mushroom stems. Reserve. Wash and dry caps, brush with melted butter. Place in a low baking dish, sprinkle with salt and pepper. Wash and dry stems. By handful, twist in the corner of a towel to extract as much moisture as possible. Chop coarsely and sauté in about 2 tablespoons of butter with scallions or shallots, salt, and pepper for 4-5 minutes or until tender.

Lower heat, add flour, mix well for about 1 minute. Stir in cream slowly, simmer until thickened a little. Add parsley.

Fill mushroom caps with the mixture, spread with a teaspoon of cheese, dribble some melted butter, and set aside until ready to cook. Bake in a preheated oven, 375 degrees, until tender (about 12-15 minutes). Serve hot, sprinkled with chopped parsley.

Number of Servings: 5-6

Frisee Salad with Kielbasa

This quick and easy salad could also be served as a dinner entrée.

½ small head curly
   endive, torn into bite
   size pieces
4 ounces beef or pork
   kielbasa, diced
1 medium shallot, minced
1 tablespoon red wine
   vinegar
3 tablespoons olive oil
   Salt and coarsely ground
   pepper
   Pear tomatoes, halved
   (optional)

Place endive in large bowl. Cook kielbasa in heavy medium skillet over medium heat until crisp, stirring frequently. Drain on paper towels. Pour off all but film of pan drippings from skillet. Add shallot to skillet and stir over medium-low heat 3 minutes. Add vinegar, scraping up browned bits. Mix in oil, salt, and pepper. Pour over salad. Add kielbasa and toss.

Number of Servings: 2

About the Wolf Trap Opera Company:

Guest artists in the early years of the company
included Beverly Sills, Roberta Peters, Norman Treigle,
Simon Estes, Evelyn Lear, and Thomas Stewart.

Veal Terrine with Mustard Sauce

A perfect hors d'oeuvre for a perfect evening.

Veal terrine:
- 2 apples, cored and quartered
- 1 medium onion, quartered
- 2 pounds ground veal
- 1 large egg, lightly beaten
- 1 teaspoon salt
- 1/4 teaspoon white pepper
- 1/4 teaspoon ground nutmeg
- 1/4 teaspoon paprika
- 1/8 teaspoon ground cinnamon
- 2 tablespoons cognac or brandy
  Vegetable cooking spray
- 1/2 cup slivered almonds
  Red Delicious apple slices

Mustard sauce:
- 1/4 cup Dijon mustard
- 1/4 cup fat free mayonnaise
- 1/4 teaspoon dried dill

Veal terrine:
Put half of the apple and onion quarters in food processor. Process 1 1/2 minutes or until smooth, stopping once to scrape down sides; transfer to a large bowl. Repeat procedure with remaining apple and onion quarters. Stir in veal and next 7 ingredients.

Spoon mixture into a 9x5x3 inch loaf pan coated with cooking spray; press into pan firmly. Sprinkle with slivered almonds. Bake at 350 degrees for 1 hour and 15 minutes. Cool in pan on wire rack. Cover and place heavy weight on top (2-3 bricks).

Refrigerate 8 hours. Slowly slide from pan and serve with apple slices and mustard sauce.

Mustard sauce:
Combine all ingredients. Cover and chill.

To serve, slice thinly and down center of loaf as well as across. Display on cutting board; arrange with fresh sage leaves, flowers, and onion slices. Put mustard sauce in attractive small pattern bowls. Top with chive flower or other edible flower. Remember a small attractive spoon for mustard sauce and a good serrated knife to slice terrine into thin slices. Serve terrine on apple slices or multigrain crackers.

Number of Servings: 8-10

Wild Rice Soup

A meal by itself! Liven by adding a little sherry at the end of cooking.

2 tablespoons butter
2 medium stalks of celery, sliced
1 medium carrot, coarsely shredded
1 medium onion, chopped (½ cup)
1 small green pepper, chopped
3 tablespoons flour
1 teaspoon salt
¼ teaspoon pepper
1½ cups cooked wild rice
2 or more cans chicken broth
1 cup half and half
⅓ cup toasted, slivered almonds
¼ cup parsley, snipped
2 plus cups of chicken, shredded (optional)

Sauté and stir celery, carrot, onion, and green pepper in butter in a 3 quart saucepan until celery is tender, about 5 minutes.

Stir in flour, salt, and pepper. Add wild rice and chicken broth.

Heat to boiling; reduce heat. Cover and simmer for 15 minutes. Stir in half and half, almonds, parsley, and chicken.

Heat just until hot; do not boil.

Number of Servings: 6

About the Wolf Trap Opera Company:

Current opera stars Stephanie Blythe, Denyce Graves, Alan Held, Nathan Gunn, and Dawn Upshaw are all Wolf Trap Opera Company alumni. Other distinguished former training program members include American Ballet Theatre Artistic Director Kevin McKenzie and actor/singer Ron Raines.

Wolf Trap Salad

The name says it all!

1 large cucumber, peeled and sliced

2 ripe tomatoes, peeled and cut into wedges

1 large green pepper, seeded and cut into wedges

1 (10 ounce) can white asparagus, drained, or fresh white asparagus, chopped

$1/2$ large (or 1 small) avocado, peeled, pitted, and sliced

Dressing:

Juice of one lemon

1 tablespoon wine or champagne vinegar

1 teaspoon dry mustard

$1/2$ teaspoon onion salt

$1/2$ tablespoon sugar

1 teaspoon dried or fresh basil, chopped

1 teaspoon dried or fresh oregano, chopped

1 teaspoon black pepper, freshly ground

$1/2$ cup salad oil

$1/2$ teaspoon fresh dill (optional)

Boston lettuce, watercress, or mixed greens

Place the cucumber slices in a bowl. Sprinkle with salt and add cold water just to cover. Refrigerate 15 minutes. Drain.

In a large plastic container or serving bowl, place in layers the tomatoes, pepper, cucumber, white asparagus, and avocado.

In a small bowl, make the dressing combining the additional ingredients, beating with a wire whisk to blend thoroughly. Pour the dressing over the vegetables. Cover and chill 1-2 hours. To distribute dressing evenly, invert the covered container several times while chilling and again just before serving.

Serve on Boston lettuce leaves, watercress, or mixed greens.

Number of Servings: 4-5

51

Avocado Soup with Crab

3 ripe avocados
1/3 cup chives, chopped
3 tablespoons lemon juice
  Salt to taste
  Fresh ground pepper
5 cups chicken broth

Topping:
1/2 cup mayonnaise
  (can use low-fat)
1 teaspoon curry powder
  Juice of 1/2 lemon
  Salt
  Fresh ground pepper
1/2 pound lump crab
  Fresh chives, minced

Put the avocados, chives, lemon juice, salt, and pepper in a food processor and process until smooth. Pour half of the chicken broth through the tube while the machine is running. Pour the soup into a bowl and whisk in the remaining broth. Cover and chill.

For the topping:
Mix together the mayonnaise, curry, lemon juice, salt, and pepper. Cover and chill until needed.

To serve:
Take the soup out of the refrigerator an hour before serving. The flavor much improves when the soup is not really cold. Season to taste. Ladle the soup into 6 bowls.

Fold the crab, with great care, into the topping mixture. Place some on the soup in each of the bowls and sprinkle with chives.

Note:
Wisdom has it that if you leave the avocado pit in the soup until served, it will stay a beautiful shade of green.

Number of Servings: 6

Norwegian Holiday Halibut

Indulge yourself with this fabulous dish! Serve with warm bread, ice cold aquavit, and beer chasers!

2 pounds of halibut
1 pound fresh asparagus, steamed
2 cups mayonnaise
1 cup whipping cream
Juice from one lemon
4 tomatoes, sliced
4 eggs, hard-boiled and sliced
$\frac{1}{2}$ pound cooked shrimp
$\frac{1}{2}$ cup chives, chopped

Simmer halibut in medium saucepan in $\frac{1}{2}$ cup of water until cooked. Let cool. Break halibut apart and spread on large platter.

Add whole cooked asparagus. Make sauce of mayonnaise, whipping cream (unwhipped), and juice from one lemon. Spread sauce over fish and asparagus. Decorate top with sliced tomatoes, sliced boiled eggs, cooked shrimp, and chives (sprinkled all over top).

Serve chilled as first course with hot bread.

Number of Servings: 10

About the Wolf Trap Opera Company:

In addition to performance experience, the Opera Company offers a series of grants to young singers for further study and career development.

White Bean and Tuna Salad

1½ cups cannellini beans
6 ounces canned solid white tuna, drained, or fresh tuna, cooked and cooled
1 tablespoon red onion, finely chopped
2 teaspoons each of basil, chives, and parsley, finely chopped
4 teaspoons red wine vinegar
3 tablespoons olive oil
Salt and pepper to taste
2 cloves garlic
½ bay leaf

Rinse and pick through the beans then soak them overnight in cold water, covering the beans by several inches.

Flake the tuna into large pieces and place in mixing bowl. In a separate bowl, mix the onion, herbs, vinegar, oil, salt, and pepper. Pour this mixture over the tuna and gently mix together. Let marinate for several hours or overnight before using. Drain the soaking liquid from the beans. Place the beans in a saucepan and cover the beans by several inches with cold water. Add the garlic and bay leaf and bring the beans to a boil over high heat. Reduce the heat to medium and cook for about 35-45 minutes or until the beans are tender, but not mushy. Remove from the heat and add salt to taste (test by tasting the cooking liquid). Cool, then refrigerate until cold.

To serve:
Using a slotted spoon, place about ¾ cup beans on each plate. Top each serving with ¼ of the tuna mixture, a healthy amount of olive oil, salt, and fresh pepper. Salad may be served on a bed of watercress or mixed greens (optional).

Number of Servings: 4

Cobb Salad

Everyone's favorite!

Salad:
- 3 avocados, diced or sliced
- 3 ounces blue cheese
- 2 hard-boiled eggs, diced or sliced
- 2$\frac{1}{2}$ cups cooked chicken, diced
- 6 slices of bacon, cooked and crumbled
- 1 head Boston lettuce
- 1 head red leafy lettuce
- 1 bunch watercress
- 12 large mushrooms, sliced
- 1 cucumber, diced or sliced
- Fresh chives
- Cherry tomatoes, halved or whole

Dressing:
- 1$\frac{1}{2}$ cups olive oil
- $\frac{2}{3}$ cup white wine vinegar
- 1 garlic clove, minced
- 1 teaspoon salt
- $\frac{1}{2}$ teaspoon black pepper
- 1 teaspoon sugar
- 1 teaspoon dry mustard
- 1 teaspoon paprika
- 1 teaspoon Worcestershire sauce

Mix all the salad ingredients into a large bowl.

Mix all the dressing ingredients well. Dress and toss salad right before serving.

Number of Servings: 6-8

Ceviche of Ahi Tuna with Mango, Pineapple, Chile, and Cilantro

A refreshing appetizer. The succulent Ahi tuna is enhanced by the sweetness of the tropical fruit, the heat of the chilies, and the aroma of fresh cilantro.

1 pound very fresh
  Ahi tuna loin
$1/4$ cup red onion, finely
  diced
1 teaspoon jalapeño, finely
  diced
1 cup mango, cut into
  $1/4$ inch pieces
1 cup pineapple cut into
  $1/4$ inch pieces
$1/4$ cup cilantro, chopped
2 limes
  Course sea salt (to taste)
  approximately $1/2$ teaspoon
  Mache lettuce
  Martini glasses for
  presentation
  Sword picks
  Toast points

Trim tuna and cut into a $1/4$ inch dice (keep cold). Dice red onion into a brunoise (very small $1/8$ inch dice). Finely chop jalapeño. Cut mango and pineapple into $1/4$ inch dice. Roughly chop cilantro (reserve some whole leaves for garnish). Place above ingredients into a medium stainless steel or glass bowl.

Squeeze in juice of two limes. Season with course sea salt to taste (approximately $1/2$ teaspoon).

Allow ceviche to chill in the refrigerator for 30 minutes before serving. Serve very cold!

Chill martini glasses in the refrigerator. To assemble, fill glasses halfway with mache lettuce. Spoon ceviche into the glass on top of the lettuce. Garnish with cilantro leaves, sword pick with $1/2$ inch chunks of mango and pineapple. Serve with warm toast points. Enjoy!

Number of Servings: 6-8 appetizer servings

FUNCTIONAL TOUCHES *can* *add* CONVENIENCE *to your kitchen.*

In most American households, the kitchen is not only a showcase for personal style, it's also the hardest working room in the home. With a wide range of accessories available, you can add finishing touches that will make your kitchen a perfect match for your needs.

To help you create a kitchen that's tailored to the way you live, following are some tips from Reico Kitchen & Bath, the leading supplier of kitchen and bath products and services in the Washington, D.C. area.

DRAWER ORGANIZATION:

- Every kitchen should have at least one four-drawer cabinet for storing flatware, cooking and baking utensils and other essentials.

- Drawer organizer kits and drawer partition kits keep tableware, large cooking utensils, serving tools, small household tools and even "junk drawer" items organized.

- Deep drawer organizers keep bulky items, such as mixing bowls and stockpots, neatly in place.

- Doors and drawers set the tone for the kitchen's design, but they should also be functional and durable. Drawers made from engineered wood and lap-joined in the corner provide adequate performance.

- Solid hardwood drawers with dovetail joints are a nice upgrade that increase the drawer's durability and add an elegant look.

More Function and Innovation tips from Reico can be found throughout the book.

Clint's Mexican Dinner

Clint Black - Country Music Performer

A delicious straightforward and easy to prepare Mexican treat.

4 ounces chicken breast, uncooked
2 teaspoons lime juice
2 tablespoons cilantro, chopped
1 tomato, chopped
$1/2$ jalapeño pepper, chopped finely
1 red onion, thinly sliced
1 green bell pepper, thinly sliced
1 red bell pepper, thinly sliced
2 corn tortillas
1 tablespoon light sour cream

Marinate chicken in 1 teaspoon lime juice and 1 tablespoon cilantro for about 1 hour.

For salsa:
Combine chopped tomato, jalapeño, 1 tablespoon cilantro, and 1 teaspoon lime juice. Set aside.

Sauté onion, green, and red bell peppers in nonstick pan with cooking spray until very soft.

Grill chicken breast for approximately 5 minutes on each side and slice into strips.

Serve with corn tortillas, sour cream, and salsa.

Add more lime and cilantro as desired for taste.

Number of Servings: 1

Rack of Lamb Crusted with Garlic and Rosemary

2 lamb racks
 (trimmed of fat)
2 tablespoons olive oil
 Sea salt and black pepper
½ cup bread crumbs
2 tablespoons parsley,
 chopped
1 tablespoon rosemary,
 chopped
1 tablespoon garlic
¾ cup extra virgin
 olive oil

Season the lamb and brush with olive oil, sea salt, and black pepper. Sear the lamb over high heat, meat-side down (should smoke) for 2-3 minutes. Place bone-side down and roast at 450 degrees for 10 minutes. Make a paste with bread crumbs and remaining ingredients. Remove meat from oven and apply breadcrumb mixture to the meat to form a crust. Return to oven for 3-4 minutes.

Serve immediately.

Number of Servings: 4

About the Filene Center:

The ground-breaking ceremony for the Filene Center at Wolf Trap National Park for the Performing Arts was attended by First Lady, Lady Bird Johnson in May 1968 along with numerous other dignitaries and celebrities.

Missy's Sweet Potato Fluff

Bruce Hornsby - Music Performer

4 cups cooked sweet
   potatoes, peeled
   and mashed
$^1/_3$ cup butter, melted
2 eggs, beaten
$^1/_2$ cup milk
1 teaspoon vanilla
$^1/_2$ cup sugar
$^1/_2$ cup pecans, chopped
$^1/_2$ cup shredded coconut
3 tablespoons butter or
   margarine, melted for
   topping

Preheat oven to 375 degrees. In a large bowl, combine mashed sweet potatoes, $^1/_3$ cup melted butter, eggs, milk, vanilla, and sugar. Spread mixture into a greased $1^1/_2$ quart casserole dish. Combine nuts, coconut, and 3 tablespoons melted butter. Sprinkle over mixture. Bake for 25 minutes.

Number of Servings: 8-10

Ratatouille

A vegetarian favorite!

4 tablespoons extra
    virgin olive oil
3 cups yellow onions,
    chopped
2 (1 pound) eggplants
    with skin on, cut into
    bite size cubes
5 garlic cloves, minced
2 green zucchini, cut into
    1 inch rounds
2 yellow zucchini, cut
    into 1 inch rounds
1 green bell pepper, cut
    into 1 inch strips
1 yellow bell pepper, cut
    into 1 inch strips
1 red pepper, cut into
    1 inch strips
2½ pounds (about 7 cups)
    ripe tomatoes, seeded
    and chopped
¼ cup fresh parsley,
    chopped
6 fresh thyme sprigs,
    chopped
2 fresh rosemary sprigs,
    chopped
2 bay leaves
½ cup fresh basil, chopped
    Salt and fresh ground
    pepper to taste

Heat olive oil in a large stock pot over medium heat. Add onion and sauté until golden, about 12 minutes; add eggplant and garlic, and sauté for 8 minutes. Add zucchini and bell peppers, and sauté for another 8 minutes. Slowly add chopped tomatoes, parsley, thyme, rosemary, and bay leaves. Cover pot and cook over low heat for 1 hour. Stir in fresh basil and add salt and fresh ground pepper to taste.

Can be prepared up to 6 hours before serving.

Delicious served at room temperature, hot or cold.

Number of Servings: 8

Shenandoah Lamb with White Bean Sauce and Salad

The perfect dish for a small intimate dinner party.

Lamb:
- 1³/4-2 pounds (8 ribs) rack of lamb, trimmed of all fat and fell (membrane) and patted dry
- ¹/4 cup olive oil
- 4 cloves garlic, peeled and minced
- 4 fresh 2 inch rosemary sprigs or 1 tablespoon dried rosemary, crumbled

Beans:
- ¹/2 pound of white beans, picked over and rinsed
- ¹/4 pound pancetta or bacon, coarsely chopped
- 1 medium onion, peeled and diced
- 1 bay leaf
- 2¹/2 quarts (10 cups) unsalted chicken stock
- 2 large cloves garlic, peeled and minced

For lamb marinade:
Place the lamb rack on a large sheet of plastic wrap and rub with olive oil. Sprinkle with garlic and arrange the rosemary sprigs over lamb. Wrap in plastic and marinate for at least four hours, or preferably, overnight in the refrigerator. Bring to room temperature before roasting.

For the beans:
Place the beans in a large bowl. Cover with enough water to come 2 inches above the beans. Cover and set aside at room temperature to soak overnight.

Place the pancetta in a heavy large pot over medium heat. Cook until browned, stirring occasionally. Add the onion, rosemary, and bay leaf; reduce heat to medium low, cover and cook until the onion is translucent, for about 10 minutes, stirring occasionally.

Drain the beans and add to the pot. Add the chicken stock and garlic. Bring to a boil skimming off any foam.

Reduce heat and simmer until the beans are very tender to taste, for about 2¹/2-3 hours, stirring occasionally, and adding more liquid if necessary.

For the bean salad:
Remove 2 cups of the beans with a slotted spoon and place in a bowl. Mix with the oil, vinegar, salt, and pepper. (This can be prepared ahead, cooled, and set aside at cool room temperature for several hours or refrigerated overnight. Bring to room temperature before serving.)

64

(continued on next page)

Shenandoah Lamb
with White Bean Sauce and Salad

Bean salad:
1 ½ tablespoons olive oil
¾ tablespoon red wine
  vinegar
  Salt and freshly ground
  black pepper to taste
4 fresh large rosemary
  sprigs for garnish
  (optional)

For the bean sauce:
Continue simmering the remaining beans for 1 hour or until almost falling apart. Transfer to a food processor using a slotted spoon. Add ¾ cup of the cooking liquid, stock, or water. Process until finely puréed, pulsing on/off and stopping to scrape down the sides of the container. Strain into small saucepan through a fine sieve, pressing on the ingredients. Add additional liquid, if necessary, to thin to a sauce-like consistency. Season with salt and pepper. (This can be prepared ahead, cooled, covered, and set aside at cool room temperature for several hours or refrigerated overnight.)

To serve:
Preheat the oven to 425 degrees. Place the lamb on a rack in a roasting pan, bone side down. Season with salt and pepper. Roast 25 minutes for rare. Let rest for 15 minutes. Slice in between ribs. Arrange the bean salad on 4 plates. Reheat the bean sauce, thinning if necessary, and ladle a large portion in the bottom. Arrange chops in pairs on each plate so that the tips meet in the center of the sauce. Place a rosemary sprig vertically between chops. Serve immediately.

Number of Servings: 4

Drunken Potatoes

This dish was discovered while dining "al-Fresco" on a quaint little island in the Exumas. The aroma is almost as good as the taste!

1 pound medium size
  white potatoes
1 can crème de coconut
½ cup coconut rum
  Ground nutmeg
  Shredded coconut

Skin the potatoes and slice them into disks. Place potatoes in a large baking dish, no lid necessary. Mix the crème de coconut and the rum. Toss the potatoes in the mixture while generously sprinkling with nutmeg.

Bake in a 350 degree oven for approximately 1½ hours.

Before serving, sprinkle the shredded coconut and more nutmeg on top of the potatoes and broil until nicely browned.

Delish!!!

Number of Servings: 6-8

About the Filene Center:

In 1973, the first official Wolf Trap Ball took place on the Filene Center stage. This sumptuous black-tie affair raises thousands of dollars for Wolf Trap Education Programs and has become a staple of the Washington social scene.

Celeriac Dauphinoise

This is a great recipe for company.

2 cups heavy cream
4 eggs
3 teaspoons salt
$^1/_2$ teaspoon pepper
4 Idaho potatoes, peeled
  and sliced
1 large celeriac, (celery
  root) approximately
  10-12 ounces
  Vegetable oil cooking
  spray
$^1/_4$ cup asiago cheese, grated
$^1/_4$ cup heavy cream,
  optional

Preheat oven to 300 degrees.

Mix together cream, eggs, salt, and pepper. Set to one side. Peel potatoes and celeriac and submerge in cold water to prevent browning. Spray a 3 quart ovenproof casserole dish with cooking spray. Slice 2 of the potatoes very thinly and layer them into the casserole dish. Top the potatoes with $^1/_2$ of the egg mixture.

Peel and slice celeriac very thinly and layer it on top of the potatoes. Slice the last two potatoes and layer on top of the celeriac. Pour the rest of the egg mixture over all. Bake in preheated oven for 1 hour and 30 minutes to 1 hour and 45 minutes.

Note:
Dauphinoise may be topped with grated asiago cheese and placed back into oven to brown top, then served immediately. To reserve, cool then refrigerate until needed. Cooled dauphinoise may be cut into shapes prior to reheating.

To reheat:
Preheat oven to 400 degrees. Cut dauphinoise into desired shapes. Pour $^1/_4$ cup heavy cream into an ovenproof casserole dish. Place dauphinoise shapes in pan. Sprinkle each with grated asiago. Place in oven 10-15 minutes or until dauphinoise is heated through and cheese on top is browned and bubbly. Serve immediately.

Number of Servings: 6-8

Cantonese Lettuce Burgers

Leonard Slatkin - Music Director,
National Symphony Orchestra

1 pound lean, finely
  ground pork (or chicken)
¹/₂ cup soy sauce
3 tablespoons sugar
2 teaspoons peanut oil
1 small can baby peas
6 water chestnuts,
  chopped
1 head lettuce (iceberg,
  red, or romaine) well
  chilled
  Fried rice (optional)

Chill wet lettuce for 5 minutes. Mix pork (or chicken) in marinade of soy sauce and sugar. In a frying pan or wok, heat the oil for 30 seconds. Cook pork (or chicken) mixture until brown. Add peas and water chestnuts. Transfer to a warm baking dish. Invite guests to serve themselves a lettuce leaf and spoon mixture into chilled lettuce leaves along with some fried rice. Then simply fold the leaf like a crepe and eat with fingers.

Number of Servings: 4-6

Chicken or Lamb Mafé

A favorite peanut butter stew within Diahanke/Manding culinary cuisine from Mali and eastern Senegal (Senegal Oriental - Tambacounda region).

2½ pounds cut chicken parts or boneless chicken (or lamb, stew cut)
1 tablespoon black ground pepper
1 teaspoon salt
3-4 tablespoons vegetable cooking oil (or olive oil)
1 medium onion, chopped
4-5 cups water
2-3 heaping tablespoons creamy peanut butter (real peanut butter without additives or sugar preferred)
1 small can tomato paste
2-3 carrots, cut in halves
1 medium cassava (yucca) root, peeled and cut into 4 pieces (or frozen cassava; substitute with 2-3 medium potatoes, skinned and cut in halves)
1-2 jumbo chicken bouillon cubes
Cayenne pepper to taste

Season the chicken or meat in a bowl with the black pepper and salt. Heat the oil in a large stewing pot (over medium heat). Add the chicken or meat to the pot with chopped onion, stirring occasionally so that it does not stick to the bottom of the pot.

As the meat begins to cook, add most of the water to the pot and let it come to a boil. (Leave some of the water to mix with the peanut butter to cream or lessen its thickness.) Stir in the peanut butter/water mixture. Let simmer a few minutes (regularly stirring to prevent sticking). Stir in the tomato paste. Add in the carrots and cassava. Crumble the bouillon cubes and add to pot. Add salt and cayenne pepper (to your desired taste; note that cayenne pepper is very hot so you may want to use a very small amount, possibly ½ teaspoon).

Half cover with lid (so that the lid covers ⅔ of the pot.) Let simmer over low heat, stirring occasionally for approximately 20 minutes or until the oil from the tomatoes starts to separate to the top of the stew.

Serve over rice or couscous.

Number of Servings: 4-6

Sautéed Shrimp and Grits

Grits:
- $1/2$ **cup white, old-fashioned grits**
- $1\,1/4$ **cup milk**
- $1\,1/4$ **cup whipping cream**
- 2 **tablespoons butter**
- 1 **teaspoon salt**

Shrimp:
- 2 **tablespoons olive oil**
- 1 **Vidalia onion, thinly sliced**
- **Salt and pepper to taste**
- 24 **fresh shrimp, peeled and deveined**
- 6 **garlic cloves, chopped**
- 6 **ounces lager beer**
- 1 **lemon, juiced**
- 1 **tablespoon fresh thyme**
- 2 **tablespoons butter**
- 1 **tomato, peeled and chopped**

Bring grits and milk to a slow boil. Simmer for 18 minutes, stirring frequently. Add heavy cream, 2 tablespoons of butter and 1 teaspoon salt.

In half of the olive oil, sauté onion until golden brown. Add salt and pepper to taste. Set aside.

In remaining olive oil sauté shrimp until cooked with a pinch of salt and pepper. Add chopped garlic and beer. Squeeze in the lemon juice and simmer for one minute. Finish sauce with fresh thyme (reserving some for garnish), 2 tablespoons butter, sautéed onions, and chopped tomato.

Divide cooked grits into serving bowls and top with shrimp and sauce. Garnish with remaining thyme and serve with a green salad.

Number of Servings: 4

Silver Queen Corn Pudding

American rustic cuisine, pure and simple.

3 cups fresh silver queen corn
6 eggs, stirred and beaten
3 cups heavy cream
$\frac{1}{2}$ cup sugar
1 teaspoon salt
1 teaspoon flour
$\frac{1}{2}$ teaspoon baking powder
2 teaspoons butter, melted

Preheat oven to 325 degrees.

Pulse corn in a food processor; drain in a colander for 1 hour. This step is very important!

Combine all ingredients, stir until well mixed. Turn into a casserole and bake $\frac{3}{4}$-$1\frac{1}{4}$ hour, depending on the casserole size. Serve warm or at room temperature.

Hint:
Frozen silver queen corn can be substituted for fresh corn.

Number of Servings: 8

Bean Chowder for Y'all

Enjoy this vegetarian recipe on a cold winter's night.

1 (30 ounce) can tomatoes, diced and puréed
$\frac{1}{4}$ cup chopped carrots
1 (26 ounce) can red kidney beans, rinsed
2 teaspoons chili powder
1 cup water
$\frac{1}{2}$ cup onions, chopped
$\frac{1}{2}$ cup green bell pepper, chopped
$\frac{1}{2}$ cup chili sauce
$\frac{1}{2}$ cup red bell pepper, chopped

Heat canned tomatoes in heavy $2\frac{1}{2}$ quart saucepan. Add other ingredients. Bring to a boil then reduce heat. Simmer 1 hour. Add a pinch of ground cumin for extra flavor.

Number of Servings: 6

Baked Eggplant and Shrimp Casserole

A delicious New Orleans inspired dish.

1 pound shrimp, peeled and boiled (save the shrimp water)

3 medium eggplants, peeled and wedged

1-2 tablespoons olive oil for sautéing

2 large celery sticks, chopped

2 medium onions, chopped

1 medium green pepper, chopped

3 teaspoons fresh parsley, chopped

1 (8 ounce) bag bread stuffing mix

1 egg lightly beaten
Salt and pepper to taste

8 raw bacon strips for topping/garnish (optional)

Boil the eggplant wedges in salted water, cutting through the pieces as they cook. Don't let them get too soft.

Sauté the celery, adding in the onions, green pepper, and parsley. When the vegetables are soft, add in the stuffing mix, eggplant, and cooked shrimp. Add the beaten egg into the mixture, keeping it soft but not too gummy. Add in some of the shrimp water if more moisture is needed. Add salt and pepper to taste.

Place mixture into a large casserole dish, and lay strips of raw bacon on top, if desired. Bake at 350 degrees until well heated, about 15-20 minutes.

Number of Servings: 4-6

Eggplant Spaghetti Sauce

Serve with a tossed salad and Italian bread for a complete meal.

1 large onion, minced
2 cloves garlic, minced
1 eggplant, peeled and cubed
2 large cans tomatoes, diced or whole
1 can tomato paste (optional)
4-5 bay leaves
¼ teaspoon basil
½ teaspoon oregano
1 (1 pound) package of angel hair pasta

Sauté onion and garlic in 2-3 tablespoons vegetable oil. Add eggplant and sauté for five minutes. After browning add tomatoes, tomato paste, and herbs. Simmer for 10 minutes.

Remove bay leaves before serving over cooked angel hair pasta.

Number of Servings: 6-8

About the Filene Center:

Renowned for its fantastic acoustics, the Filene Center has been the site of several live recordings by artists including Arlo Guthrie, Pete Seeger, Judy Collins, and The Doobie Brothers.

Zucchini Bread Pudding

4 cups challah bread,
unsliced, crusts removed
and cut into 1 inch cubes
6 tablespoons butter
1 cup onion, chopped
2 pounds small zucchini,
halved lengthwise and
cut into $1/2$ inch half
rounds
2 eggs
1 teaspoon dried oregano
$3/4$ teaspoon salt
$1/2$ teaspoon fresh ground
pepper
Pinch cayenne pepper
1 cup milk
$1^1/2$ cups jack cheese, grated

Preheat oven to 375 degrees. Grease a 2 quart shallow baking dish.

Melt 4 tablespoons of the butter. Pat the bread cubes in the prepared dish and drizzle the melted butter over the top. Bake until the edges of the bread cubes begin to brown lightly, 12-15 minutes, stirring once. Set aside.

Melt the remaining 2 tablespoons butter in a large skillet over medium heat. Add the onion and cook until soft, about 5 minutes. Add the zucchini and cook, stirring now and then, until soft, about 8 minutes. Set aside to cool slightly.

In a large bowl, beat the eggs with the oregano, salt, pepper, and cayenne pepper. Whisk in the milk. Gently stir the cooled zucchini mixture into the eggs and then pour it over the toasted bread cubes. Gently stir the two together a bit. Strew the grated cheese over the top. (The bread pudding can now be baked, or even better, covered and chilled for 4 hours or even overnight. Take it out of the refrigerator about an hour before baking.)

Bake until the filling is set and the top browned a bit, about 35-40 minutes. Serve hot.

Number of Servings: 8

Wild Rice Pancakes

These are wonderful as a main dish or served alongside salmon or chicken.

½ cup wild rice
⅔ cup water
1 teaspoon salt
¾ cup carrot, finely diced
¾ cup celery, finely diced
1½ cups red onion,
   finely chopped
⅓ cup green onions,
   chopped (use entire stem)
¾ teaspoon fresh parsley,
   chopped
¾ teaspoon fresh thyme,
   chopped
4 tablespoons unsalted
   butter
2 eggs
¾ cup whole milk
1 cup flour
   Fresh ground pepper
   and salt to taste
   Vegetable oil

In a heavy saucepan combine the rice, water, and salt. Simmer covered for 50-60 minutes or until all water is absorbed. Set rice aside in a large mixing bowl and let cool. In a sauté pan cook the carrot, celery, onion, green onion, parsley, and thyme in the butter over medium heat until tender, about 15 minutes; stir occasionally. Once cooked, transfer the mixture into the rice.

In a small bowl whisk together the eggs and milk. Stir the egg mixture into the rice and then stir in the flour with fresh ground pepper and salt to taste.

Heat a griddle over very high heat until hot. Brush with vegetable oil, or spray pan with vegetable cooking oil spray. In batches, scoop the batter onto the griddle by ¼ cup measures. Flatten the pancakes with a spoon and cook them for 3-4 minutes per side, or until they are golden brown. Transfer the pancakes to a baking sheet or ovenproof platter, and keep warm in a preheated 200 degree oven, until ready to serve.

Number of Servings: 20

John's Family Pierogies

John Gorka - Folk Music Performer

This recipe comes from the Gorka (Polish) side of John's family, as adapted by his Italian mom. Traditionally, they served it on special occasions with champagne as the only accompaniment.

Potato Cheese Filling:
- 2 **medium potatoes (peeled and boiled)**
- 3 **tablespoons half and half**
- 1 **pound ricotta cheese**
  Scallions, chopped fine (buy a bunch; use half here and half for sauerkraut-bacon filling below)
- 3 **large cloves garlic, minced**
  Dried basil (lots)
  Black pepper
  Dried oregano (little bit)
  Salt (not too much)

Sauerkraut and bacon filling:
- 4 **whole strips of bacon**
- 1 **can Bavarian-style kraut, strained to remove liquid**
  Scallions, chopped fine
- 3 **large cloves garlic, minced**

Filling:
For potato-cheese filling, mash potatoes together with the half and half, mix with cheese. Add scallions and garlic, spices to taste.

Sauerkraut-bacon filling:
Fry bacon, put on paper towels to drain grease. Meanwhile, put strained sauerkraut into small frying/sauté pan. Cut or tear bacon into small bits, then add the bits to the pan with sauerkraut. Add chopped scallions and garlic. Simmer until sauerkraut is translucent and a little brown. Let cool.

Dough:
Mix flour and salt in a big bowl. Make a well in the middle of the flour for the butter and eggs, then put them in. Using a spoon, stir up the mixture slowly, adding warm water to make a stiff dough (You may not need all the water.) Now knead dough until very smooth. Let stand in bowl for 10 minutes covered by a clean dish towel. (Don't let it sit too long or it will be harder to roll out.)

Lightly flour work surface (e.g. a large cutting board on a table). Divide dough in half leaving one half covered in bowl. Take the other half and shape by working out from the center with a roller to make a rectangle $1/16$ inch thick.

(continued on next page)

John's Family Pierogies

Dough:
- 3 cups flour
- $\frac{1}{4}$ teaspoon salt
- 2 tablespoons butter, cut into pieces
- 2 eggs
- 1 cup warm water

Assemble pierogies:

Using a knife or a pizza cutter, score the dough rectangle horizontally across the middle. Place spoonfuls of sauerkraut-bacon filling onto dough below score line, spacing evenly to get 3 rows of 5 or 6 (use approximately 1 tablespoon filling for each pierogi, gently squeezing to remove excess moisture before placing on dough). Fold top half of dough down over bottom half. Press dough around the little mounds and cut into individual square pierogies. (You may need lots of flour to keep from sticking.) Press edges down with your fingers at first, then with a fork. Put pierogies on floured paper towels.

Repeat using reserved half of dough and potato-cheese filling. (You'll probably have leftover potato cheese filling after you're done.)

Bring big pots of water to boil, adding some olive oil and salt. Gently but quickly add pierogies by hand. Bring back to a gentle boil and cook, stirring occasionally for a total cooking time of no more than 10 minutes. Serve with melted butter, salt, and pepper.

Number of Servings: 8

Sausage and Beans

A great summer family get-together recipe. Make early in the morning when the house is cool and reheat when the family is hungry. Real comfort food!

1 $\frac{1}{2}$ quarts (2 $\frac{1}{2}$ pounds) dry kidney beans
4 $\frac{1}{2}$ gallons boiling water
1 tablespoon garlic, minced
1 quart onion, chopped
1 $\frac{1}{2}$ cups green pepper, chopped
4 pounds sausage or hamburger
2 tablespoons salt
2 tablespoons chili powder
2 quarts canned tomatoes
1 quart bean liquid (reserved)
$\frac{1}{2}$ cup flour

Add dry beans to boiling water, boil for 2 minutes. Remove from heat and let beans soak for 1 hour. Cook beans in soaking liquid about 1 hour. The beans will be slightly underdone. Drain beans and save liquid.

Sauté garlic, onion, green pepper, and sausage (or hamburger) until slightly brown. Add beans to the cooked mix.

Stir in salt, chili powder, tomatoes, reserved bean liquid, and flour. Stir well. Simmer until thickened (about 30 minutes).

Serve with cornbread and more chopped sweet onion.

Number of Servings: 25 - 1 cup servings

About the Filene Center:

Leonard Bernstein celebrated his 60th birthday by conducting a National Symphony Orchestra performance at Wolf Trap in 1978. André Previn, Yehudi Menuhin, Mstislav Rostropovich, Aaron Copland, and over 50 other performers were part of this televised celebration.

Chilaquiles with Chipotle Sour Cream Sauce

18 white or yellow corn
   tortillas, 6 inch diameter,
   cut into 8 triangles
   Canola oil

Chipotle sauce:
   6 large garlic cloves, whole
   2 small onions, peeled and
      cut into quarters
   4 pounds tomatoes, cut
      into quarters
   6 canned chipotle chilies
   3 tablespoons canola oil
      Salt to taste
   4 fresh oregano sprigs
   1/2 cup fresh cilantro,
      chopped
   1 cup sour cream
   1/2 cup red onion, chopped
   1 cup queso fresco
      (Mexican cheese or
      substitute with farmer's
      cheese)

For chilaquiles:
Pour enough canola oil in a large skillet to reach a
depth of 1 inch. Heat oil over medium high heat.
Add 8 tortilla triangles at a time to the oil and fry,
turning occasionally, until golden, about one minute.
Using tongs or a slotted spoon transfer the triangles
to paper towels to drain off excess oil and to cool.

For chipotle sauce:
In a large sauté pan heat 1 tablespoon of canola oil,
place garlic and onion in skillet and cook until onion
becomes browned. Transfer the onion and garlic to a
mixing bowl.

Using the same sauté pan, heat 1 tablespoon of
canola oil. Working in batches cook the tomatoes
until skins begin to brown, turning occasionally,
about 30 minutes. Repeat step with another batch of
the tomatoes. Transfer the cooked tomatoes to onion
and garlic mixture. Place the tomatoes, onion, garlic,
and chipotle chilies into the bowl of a food processor
and process until smooth.

Heat 1 tablespoon of the canola oil in a deep sauté
pan over medium high heat, add tomato mixture to
pan. (Note the mixture will bubble very quickly.)
Stir in salt and simmer until sauce thickens, stirring
frequently, for about 20 minutes. Add oregano and
stir in tortilla chips. Immediately divide tortilla chips
on 6 plates. Top with cilantro, sour cream, chopped
onion, and queso fresco.

Serve with your favorite cerveza, a squeeze of fresh
lime and enjoy!

Number of Servings: 6

Jumbo Lump Crab Cakes with Rémoulade

Chef's Best Recipe

Brian McBride, Executive Chef

Melrose Restaurant
Park Hyatt Hotel
1201 24th Street, NW
Washington, DC 22037

Rémoulade:

- 2 cups prepared mayonnaise
- 2 anchovy fillets, fresh or canned (rinse to remove excess salt), chopped (optional)
- 1/4 cup fresh Italian parsley, chopped
- 1/3 cup cornichons
  Juice of 1/2 lemon (about 1 1/2 tablespoons)
- 1 tablespoon capers, drained
- 2 drops hot sauce
- 1 teaspoon Worcestershire sauce
- 1 clove garlic, minced

Rémoulade:

Combine all ingredients in a medium bowl and whisk together. Refrigerate until needed; the rémoulade will keep for 1 week or more if refrigerated in an airtight container.

Crab cakes:

Pick over the crab meat for shells and discard them, being careful not to break up the lumps of crab meat. Put in a mixing bowl and set aside. In another mixing bowl, combine the mustard, eggs, parsley, hot sauce, and Worcestershire, whisk together, and season with salt and pepper. Pour the egg mixture over the crab meat and gently combine with your hands, taking care not to break up the chunks of crab meat. Gently fold in the bread crumbs. The crab cake mixture should be loose and wet, not dry. Mold the mixture into sixteen 3 1/2 ounce crab cakes and refrigerate until serving time. When almost ready to serve, preheat the oven to 400 degrees. Divide the clarified butter between two sauté pans and heat over medium heat. When the butter is

(continued on next page)

82

Jumbo Lump Crab Cakes with Rémoulade

Crab Cakes:

- **3 pounds jumbo lump crab meat**
- **2 tablespoon Dijon mustard**
- **3 large eggs**
- **¼ cup fresh Italian parsley, chopped**
- **3 drops hot sauce**
- **1 teaspoon Worcestershire sauce**
- **Salt and freshly ground pepper to taste**
- **¾ cup fresh white bread crumbs**
- **¼ cup clarified butter or extra virgin olive oil**
- **Grilled vegetables (optional)**

hot, add the crab cakes and cook for about 2 minutes on each side until browned. Place on baking sheet and transfer to the oven until cooked through, about 10 minutes.

Arrange with grilled vegetables on warm dinner plates and place 2-3 crab cakes on each plate. Serve the rémoulade on the side. Serve with watercress salad (see page 31.)

Number of Servings: 5-8

Cold Spaghetti with Littleneck Clams and Osetra Caviar

This is an absolutely perfect dish to enjoy during the summer because of its refreshing taste. Since the pasta is cold, one is able to enjoy each element of the recipe to the fullest.

$2^1/2$ pounds littleneck clams
$1^3/4$ cups white wine
2 garlic cloves
6 tablespoons extra virgin olive oil
Juice of $1/2$ lemon
Salt and pepper
$1/2$ pound dry spaghetti extra fine
$1/2$ bunch chives
$1^1/2$ ounces Osetra Caviar

Clams:
Rinse clams in cold water and then strain. Repeat 3-4 times or until water becomes clear. After the final strain, have the garlic cloves and the white wine ready. Place a small saucepan on stove. When it reaches its top heat, add clams followed by wine, garlic, and 3 tablespoons of olive oil. Cover saucepan with lid and cook clams until completely open. Transfer clams to a large tray, shell, and strain and reserve all of the cooking juices. Keep refrigerated.

Clam dressing:
Warm lemon juice and place it in a bowl and add the same amount of clam juice. Add a pinch of salt and whisk with the remaining olive oil. Set dressing aside until you are ready to toss it in the pasta.

Finishing and presentation:
Thinly slice chives and put aside. Cook pasta in salted boiling water for approximately $2^1/2$ minutes. Strain and chill in iced salted water. Strain a second time and dry excess water with a kitchen cloth. Place pasta in bowl with clam dressing, along with chives and clam meat. Strain excess clam juice from bowl after mixing pasta with a chef's fork. Twirl spaghetti on plate and garnish with caviar (enough for all plates to have same amount).

Number of Servings: 4

Avocado Stuffed Swordfish

Tom Smothers - Folk Musician and Comedian

Rowan and Martin were a classic comedy team and our friends. My favorite recipe comes from Dan Rowan's daughter-in-law, Marla Rowan. This has been our favorite family recipe for years.

2 swordfish steaks, at least one inch thick
1 ripe avocado, mashed
2 garlic cloves, crushed
2 tablespoons onion, minced
2 tablespoons lemon juice
1 teaspoon Worcestershire sauce
3 tablespoons butter, melted
1/3 cup soy sauce
1/4 cup lemon juice
1/2 cup vegetable oil
2 teaspoons Dijon mustard

Cut a pocket in swordfish steaks. In medium size bowl, mix avocado, garlic, onion, 2 tablespoons lemon juice, Worcestershire sauce, and butter. Stuff mixture into each of the pockets using broken toothpicks if necessary to keep mixture in place.

Mix soy sauce, 1/4 cup lemon juice, oil, and mustard together. Pour over swordfish and let marinate 1-2 hours. Grill or broil until done, usually 8-10 minutes or 4-5 minutes per side.

Enjoy!

Number of Servings: 2

Garlic Pork Roast

This is a quick all-in-one dinner. Adding a salad of your choice on the side with rolls finishes the meal. Easy clean up and great leftovers!

2 pounds boneless rolled
   pork loin roast
9 garlic cloves (or to taste)
1 small onion, quartered
6-8 new potatoes with
   skin left on, halved
6 large carrots, peeled
   and sliced
1 tablespoon
   Worcestershire sauce
$\frac{1}{2}$ teaspoon pepper
$\frac{1}{2}$ teaspoon salt
1 tablespoon flour
6 ounces beer
   Fresh parsley for
   garnish (optional)

With a knife, make slits in pork roast and insert garlic. Place roast in medium size roasting pan. Add remaining ingredients in order listed, except beer.

Pour beer over ingredients.

Bake at 350 degrees for 3 hours, turning vegetables every $\frac{1}{2}$ hour. Cover for first two hours; uncover for final hour.

Serve pork roast sliced on platter surrounded by vegetables. Garnish with fresh parsley.

Number of Servings: 4-6

About the Filene Center:

Legendary entertainer Bob Hope was the Master of Ceremonies at Wolf Trap's Tenth Anniversary Gala in 1981, bringing his trademark wit and laughter to this historic event.

Capellini with Sausage and Spinach

The ingredients create their own sauce as they cook together. Be sure to have plenty of garlic bread to accompany this delicious dish.

2 teaspoons olive oil
1 pound sweet Italian
  sausage, cut into
  $1/2$ inch thick slices
1 large onion, chopped
2 large garlic cloves,
  chopped
3 (14 ounce) cans
  chicken broth
$1/4$ cup water
8 ounces capellini or
  vermicelli pasta,
  broken in half
2 bags (10 ounces each)
  spinach, coarsely
  chopped
$1/4$ teaspoon ground pepper
$1/4$ teaspoon salt
$1/4$ teaspoon chili powder
$1/2$ cup heavy or whipping
  cream (optional)

Heat oil in a Dutch oven or stockpot over medium high heat; add sausage and cook 3-4 minutes, turning as it browns. Add onion and garlic, cook 2-3 minutes until lightly browned. Add broth and water to pot. Cover and bring to a boil. Add pasta and cook 3 minutes, stirring frequently. Add spinach, salt, pepper, and chili powder, stirring the spinach into the pasta and sauce, 2-3 minutes, until pasta is al denté and spinach is wilted. Stir in cream. Serve immediately.

Number of Servings: 4-6

Beef Stroganoff

A delicious favorite.

2 large onions, sliced finely
2-3 tablespoons butter
2 pounds tender beef
   (or veal cutlet)
$\frac{1}{4}$ tablespoon paprika
1 tablespoon parsley,
   chopped
1 cup beef broth
1 tablespoon flour
$\frac{1}{4}$ small can tomato paste
   Juice of $\frac{1}{2}$ lemon
3 cups mushrooms, gently
   washed and sliced
1 cup sour cream
   Salt and pepper to taste
   Egg noodles, cooked

In a large saucepan, sauté onions with salt and pepper in butter slowly until golden. Cut meat in even slices (remove all tendons and fat), and sprinkle with salt and pepper. Add beef to sauté pan and smother with onions, paprika, and chopped parsley. Cover for 15-20 minutes.

Meanwhile, mix warm broth with flour then tomato paste and lemon juice. Add to meat and let simmer covered for 10-20 minutes.

Sauté mushrooms in butter with salt, pepper, and parsley and add to meat in last 2 minutes of cooking.

Just before serving add sour cream.

Reheat and serve with chopped parsley and egg noodles.

Number of Servings: 6-8

Cranberry Fluff

Try this for an easy accompaniment to your traditional turkey dinner.

2 cups raw cranberries
3 cups miniature
   marshmallows
¾ cup sugar
2 cups chopped apples
½ cup seedless grapes,
   halved
½ cup toasted pecans
1 cup whipped cream

Grind cranberries in food processor. Combine cranberries, marshmallows, and sugar and put in refrigerator overnight. Add chopped apples, grapes, and toasted pecans. Fold in whipped cream.

Serve immediately.

Number of Servings: 8-10

About the Filene Center:

Between 1938 and 1946, Catherine Filene Shouse hosted an annual "Have-Fun Carnival" at her farm in June. Guests purchased 20 tickets for a dollar which included parking, supper, mint juleps, games, and a chance to dance with "Dime-a-Dance-Girls." Numerous distinguished Congressmen and Cabinet members took part in the carnival, acting in the sideshow and as carnival barkers.

Pecan-Breaded Chicken Breasts with Dijon Mustard Sauce

Finely ground pecans are used instead of flour to coat these savory chicken breasts. The resulting flavor and texture are irresistible.

8 tablespoons (1 stick) butter
3 tablespoons Dijon mustard
6 ounces pecans, finely ground (about 1½ cups)
1 tablespoon vegetable oil
8 skinless, boneless chicken breast halves, pounded to ¼ inch thickness
⅔ cup sour cream
½ teaspoon salt
¼ teaspoon freshly ground pepper

In a small saucepan, melt 6 tablespoons of the butter, whisk in 2 tablespoons of the mustard until blended. Scrape into a shallow dish. Place pecans in another shallow dish.

Spread butter and mustard mixture on both sides of the chicken, dredge in pecans to coat.

In a large frying pan, heat remaining 2 tablespoons butter in vegetable oil over medium heat. Add chicken and cook 3 minutes per side, until lightly browned and tender. Remove to a serving platter and cover with foil to keep warm.

Discard all but 2 tablespoons of fat from pan and reduce heat to low. Add sour cream and whisk in remaining tablespoon mustard, salt, and pepper. Blend well. Cook until heated through; do not boil. Serve over chicken.

Number of Servings: 8

BBQ Beef Brisket

Comfort food!

1 whole fresh beef brisket
  (not corned beef)
2 bay leaves
  Dash of liquid smoke
1/4 cup dry onion flakes
  Salt and pepper to taste
  BBQ sauce (see recipe
  on page 183)

Place brisket in center of large sheet of foil. Top with bay leaves, liquid smoke, onion flakes, salt, and pepper. Fold foil tightly over the meat. Place in 250 degree oven. Bake approximately 1 hour per pound in a very slow oven or until fork tender. Remove and cool until easily sliced very thin (several hours in the refrigerator).

Cover with favorite BBQ sauce and reheat until hot through.

Number of Servings: 6-8

About the Filene Center:

The Filene Center is thirteen stories high. The enormous backstage space contains extensive rigging to accommodate massive set changes.

Lemon and Herb Rock Cornish Hens

Does not matter how old or proper—no one eats this fabulous tasting dish without licking their fingers!

4 teaspoons fresh oregano, chopped
4 teaspoons fresh thyme, chopped
4 teaspoons fresh rosemary, chopped
4-8 cloves garlic, chopped
1 teaspoon salt
1 cup lemon juice
1/2 cup olive oil
3 large Cornish hens, split, back bone removed

Mince all herbs and garlic. A mini chopper will work well. Whisk herbs and garlic with olive oil and lemon juice. Place hens in a ceramic dish large enough to lay out flat. Pour marinade over hens and marinate in refrigerator overnight. Drain the hens but save the marinade.

Grill the hens 17-20 minutes, basting with the marinade. Grill until the juices are clear and skin is nicely browned.

Serve garnished with fresh rosemary, oregano, and/or thyme sprigs.

Delicious hot or at room temperature.

Number of Servings: 4-6

About the Filene Center:

Many legends of music and the performing arts have graced the Filene Center stage. Sammy Davis, Jr., Ella Fitzgerald, Miles Davis, Mikhail Baryshnikov, Aaron Copland, the Metropolitan Opera, Bill Cosby, and Bob Dylan are just a few of the world-renowned stars who have performed at Wolf Trap.

Lentil Stew with Mint and Lemon

Serve this stew with your favorite crusty bread.

3 tablespoons olive oil
3 large garlic cloves, chopped
1 cup lentils, rinsed and picked over
2 tablespoons fresh parsley, chopped
3 cups canned vegetable broth
8 ounces red potatoes, skinned and cut into $1/2$ inch pieces
1 lemon
8 ounces (about 9 cups) fresh spinach, torn into pieces
$1/4$ teaspoon paprika
$1/4$ teaspoon cayenne pepper
$1/4$ cup fresh mint
    Salt and pepper to taste
    Feta cheese (optional)

Heat olive oil in a large saucepan over medium heat. Add garlic and sauté until golden. Add lentils, chopped parsley, and vegetable broth to remainder of garlic and onion mixture and bring to a low boil. Reduce heat, cover and simmer 15 minutes. Add potato pieces and cook until lentils and potatoes are tender, stirring occasionally, about 20 minutes.

Grate lemon peel from lemon (about $1/2$ of a teaspoon) and squeeze juice from the lemon to measure 3 tablespoons. Add lemon peel, juice, torn spinach, paprika, and cayenne pepper to the stew. Simmer in covered pot until spinach is wilted, about 3 minutes. Stir in fresh mint and season to taste with salt and pepper.

Serve stew in large soup bowls and top with crumbled feta cheese.

Number of Servings: 2

93

Fire and Ice Chili à la Rogers

Kenny Rogers - Country Music Performer

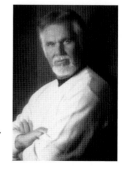

*I'm pleased to share one of my very favorite recipes with you.
You have to taste my Fire and Ice Chili to believe how delicious it is.
This chili warms a Southern boy's heart and soul.*

1 (20 ounce) can pineapple chunks in syrup
1 (28 ounce) can whole tomatoes, with juice
1 (6 ounce) can tomato paste
1 (4 ounce) can green chilies, diced
3 cloves garlic, pressed or minced
2 medium-size yellow onions, chopped
1 green bell pepper, seeded and chopped
1/4 cup chili powder
4 teaspoons ground cumin
1 tablespoon jalapeño chilies, diced (for more fire, add 2 tablespoons jalapeño chilies)
2 teaspoons salt
2 tablespoons olive oil
2 pounds lean boneless pork butt, cut into 1 inch cubes

Condiments:
Small bowls of sliced green onions, shredded cheddar cheese, and sour cream

Drain pineapple, reserving syrup. Drain and chop tomatoes, reserving juice. In large bowl, combine reserved syrup, tomatoes and juice, tomato paste, green chilies, 2 cloves garlic, 1 onion, bell pepper, chili powder, cumin, jalapeño chilies, and salt.

Heat olive oil in Dutch oven until very hot. Brown pork on all sides in batches. (Don't overcrowd pot. Add just enough pork to cover bottom.) With all browned pork in pot, add remaining garlic and onion. Cook until onion is soft. Add tomato mixture to pork mixture. Cover and simmer 3 hours, stirring occasionally. Add pineapple for the last 30 minutes of cooking. Serve with condiments.

Happy eating!

Number of Servings: 8-10

Lemon Parmesan Chicken

Serve with white rice or angel hair pasta and your favorite green vegetable. Enjoy!

8 chicken cutlets
1 cup milk
1 cup bread crumbs
1 cup grated Parmesan cheese
2 tablespoons parsley, chopped
1 cup olive oil
Salt and pepper
1 lemon, thinly sliced
1 cup white wine
¼ cup lemon juice
1 cup chicken broth
Triple sec or orange liqueur

Soak chicken in milk for about 10 minutes. Mix bread crumbs, Parmesan cheese, chopped parsley and dredge each slice of chicken in mixture. Add olive oil to a large skillet and quickly cook chicken on each side until lightly browned. Do not overcook. Place the chicken in a lightly buttered baking dish and lightly salt and pepper. Place one slice of lemon on top of each piece of chicken. Remove all but one tablespoon oil from skillet, leaving residue from chicken. Add white wine and boil until liquid is reduced by half. Add lemon juice and chicken broth, boil until liquid is reduced by half and pour over chicken slices. Drizzle triple sec or orange liqueur over each slice of chicken. Bake at 350 degrees until liquid begins to bubble, 20-25 minutes.

Number of Servings: 8

About the Filene Center:

In 1974, Wolf Trap started producing *In Performance at Wolf Trap* with WETA public television. Hosted by Beverly Sills, it was the first televised arts series to originate in the U.S. and featured such talents as Benny Goodman, Martha Graham Dance Company, Sarah Vaughan, the National Symphony Orchestra, and Wolf Trap Opera Company.

Braised Lamb Shanks with Rosemary

6 lamb shanks
(1 pound each)
2 tablespoons olive oil
2 medium onions, chopped
3 large carrots, peeled and
cut into $1/4$ inch slices
10 cloves garlic, smashed
1 bottle dry red wine
1 (28 ounce) can diced
tomatoes with juices
1 (12 ounce) can chicken
broth
1 (12 ounce) can beef broth
5 teaspoons fresh rosemary,
chopped, plus some
branches for decoration
1 teaspoon dried thyme
2 teaspoons lemon peel,
grated

Preheat broiler and place a shelf 4 inches below the flame. Put the shanks in a foil lined pan. Rub them all over with 1 tablespoon of oil and sprinkle with salt and pepper. Broil until browned on both sides, about 6 minutes per side. Set them aside. Lower oven to 350 degrees.

Heat on stove the remaining tablespoon oil in a large casserole that will hold the shanks and vegetables. Add the onions, carrots, and garlic and sauté until golden, about 10 minutes. Stir in the remaining ingredients and shanks, pressing them down to submerge. Bring the liquids to a boil. Cover the pot and bake until the meat is tender, about 2 hours.

Uncover the pot and bake 30 minutes more, or until the meat is very tender.

Remove the shanks from the pot. Bring the juices to a boil and cook for 15 minutes, until they are reduced and thickened. Season with salt and pepper. Return the lamb to the casserole, let cool and then cover and chill. May be done a few days ahead.

To serve:
Bring the casserole up to room temperature and then heat in a 350 degree oven until very hot, about 30 minutes. Place the shanks on individual plates and spoon on some of the juices. Decorate with branches of rosemary. Serve with baked polenta or rice.

Number of Servings: 6

Herb and Garlic-Crusted Beef Tenderloin

Uncork a bottle of your favorite red wine and enjoy.

8 tablespoons olive oil
2 (2½ pound) pieces beef tenderloin (thick end), trimmed
6 garlic cloves, minced
2½ tablespoons fresh thyme, minced
2½ tablespoons fresh parsley, chopped
2½ tablespoons fresh rosemary, minced
6 tablespoons Dijon mustard

Preheat oven to 375 degrees. Rub 1 tablespoon oil over each beef piece. Sprinkle with salt and pepper. Heat 2 large nonstick skillets over high heat. Add 1 beef piece to each; brown on all sides, about 5 minutes.

Place beef pieces in large roasting pan. Mix 6 tablespoons oil, garlic, 2 tablespoons thyme, 2 tablespoons parsley, and 2 tablespoons rosemary in small bowl.

Coat top and sides of beef pieces with mustard, then with herb mixture. Roast until meat thermometer inserted into center of beef registers 125 degrees. For medium-rare, about 45 minutes. Transfer to platter. Let stand 10 minutes.

Cut beef into ½-inch thick slices. Sprinkle with remaining ½ teaspoon each of thyme, parsley, and rosemary.

Number of Servings: 10

Veal Marengo

This dish comes from a small town in Northern Italy where Napoleon won a historic battle. Being in good spirits and very hungry, he told his chef to prepare an especially good dinner. The chef in the war-beaten country could not find any other ingredients except these that made the Veal Marengo famous. Chicken may be prepared in the same way.

2 pounds veal or chicken, cut into cubes (no fat or tendons)

¼ teaspoon marjoram or oregano

Salt, pepper, and paprika

½ cup oil or butter

1 large onion, peeled and sliced

2 tablespoons flour

2 cups veal or chicken broth

¾ cup dry white wine or sherry

1 bouquet garni*

1 clove garlic, mashed

2 tablespoons parsley, chopped

1 pound tomatoes, peeled, seeded, and diced

2 cups mushrooms, peeled, sliced

Bread for croutons, 1 per person, triangle shape

Butter to sauté croutons

Hard-boiled eggs, sliced

Rub veal with a light dusting of marjoram or oregano. Heat oil to medium-high in a large skillet and put in meat. The pieces should have space, so if the skillet is not big enough, proceed twice. Cook meat until yellow-gold, remove oil, add salt, pepper, paprika, onion, and flour, sauté until flour becomes yellow. Add broth, wine, bouquet, garlic, parsley, and tomatoes. Cover and simmer in a 300-350 degree oven for 1 hour.

Remove meat, blend sauce in blender. It should have reduced by half of its content. Put meat in ovenware serving dish, pour over sauce, put in mushrooms, check seasoning, cover, and cook for 20 minutes more. Remove bouquet garni. Serve garnished with parsley, paprika, croutons, and sliced hard-boiled eggs.

Number of Servings: 6-8

*Parsley, thyme, and bay leaf tied into a cheesecloth bag for easy removal

Egg and Cheese Soufflé

16 slices sandwich bread,
   (crusts removed)
 1 pound cheddar cheese,
   grated
12 eggs
 2 pints milk
 2 teaspoons salt
 1 cup melted butter

Layer bread on greased 9x13 casserole dish. Sprinkle half cheese on top. Beat eggs with milk and salt. Put half over cheese in casserole. Pour half cup butter over casserole.

Repeat the above to create a second layer.

Let sit in refrigerator overnight.

Bake 45 minutes in 350 degree oven. When baking, put cookie sheet under casserole as it will cook over sometimes.

Number of Servings: 6-8

About the Filene Center:

The Filene Center has one of the largest theatrical stages in the country. Its stage size is second only to the Metropolitan Opera's.

Indonesian Pork Tenderloin

Keith Lockhart - Conductor,
Boston Pops Esplanade Orchestra

Great with mashed potatoes! Can easily be doubled.

1 (1 pound) pork
  tenderloin
2 tablespoons soy sauce
2 tablespoons peanut
  butter
1 teaspoon crushed red
  pepper
2 cloves garlic, minced
1/2 cup pineapple, peach,
  or apricot preserves

Preheat oven to 375 degrees. Trim fat from tenderloin. Combine soy sauce and next 3 ingredients in mixing bowl, stirring well. Spread mixture over tenderloin in greased pan. Bake uncovered for 30 minutes. Brush tenderloin with preserves and bake an additional 10 minutes or until meat thermometer reads between 150 and 160 degrees, basting often with preserves. Let stand for 10 minutes before slicing.

Number of Servings: 4

Crab Imperial

Imperial and superb, simply delicious!

2 pounds crabmeat, back
   fin or jumbo lump
2 teaspoons pimento,
   chopped
2 teaspoons whole capers
1 teaspoon Worcestershire
   sauce
1 teaspoon salt
½ cup mayonnaise
   Splash of hot sauce
   (optional)
   Paprika

Blend seasonings into mayonnaise; pour over the crabmeat and toss together lightly. Place the crab mixture on scallop shells or small cooking dish and top off with an additional tablespoon of mayonnaise. Sprinkle with paprika. Bake at 375 degrees for 20 minutes.

Number of Servings: 4-6

About the Filene Center:

The first performance held at the Filene Center, a concert by the National Symphony Orchestra led by Julius Rudel with soloists Van Cliburn and Norman Treigle, was on July 1, 1971.

Spinach Strata

2 loaves thin sliced white
  bread (remove crusts)

Step 1 mixture:
  3 packages chopped frozen
    spinach, defrosted and
    well drained
  4 tablespoons onions,
    chopped
$2^{1}/_{2}$ cups shredded
    cheddar cheese
$1^{3}/_{4}$ tablespoons fresh
    lemon juice

Step 2 mixture:
  12 ounces sliced mozzarella
  2 medium cans tomatoes,
    sliced and drained
  3-4 (4 ounce) cans sliced
    mushrooms or fresh
    mushrooms, sliced and
    sautéed

Step 3 mixture:
  10 eggs slightly beaten
  6 cups milk
  2 teaspoons salt
  1 teaspoon oregano
  $^{1}/_{4}$ teaspoon garlic powder
  $^{1}/_{2}$ cup grated Parmesan
    cheese

Butter bottom of two 9x13 inch pans or one 15x18 inch pan. Cover bottom with some of the bread slices and spread step 1 mixture on top. Add second layer of bread, mozzarella cheese, and remaining ingredients of step 2. Add third layer of bread. Pour egg mixture of step 3 over all and sprinkle with generous amount of Parmesan cheese. Refrigerate, covered, overnight. Bake uncovered at 325 degrees for 1 hour and 15 minutes. Sprinkle with additional Parmesan before serving.

Number of Servings: 20

Sensational Seafood Casserole

A celebration by itself!

1 pound scallops
1 cup dry white wine
2 teaspoons lemon juice
2 tablespoons parsley,
  chopped
6 tablespoons butter
$1/3$ cup flour
$2 1/4$ cups heavy cream
$1/4$ cup cognac
1 tablespoon
  Worcestershire sauce
$1/3$ cup Parmesan cheese
  Salt and pepper to taste
2 egg yolks, beaten
1 pound mushrooms,
  cooked and sliced
1 pound lobster, cooked
1 pound crabmeat
1 pound shrimp, cooked
1 cup soft bread crumbs
  tossed with melted butter
  Additional cheese and
  paprika for topping
  (optional)

Cook scallops in 1 cup dry white wine with lemon juice and parsley for 3-5 minutes. Do not overcook. Drain scallops and reserve $3/4$ cup cooking liquid.

Melt the butter and add flour. Gradually stir in reserved scallop liquid, cream, cognac, and Worcestershire sauce. Cook until thickened. Add cheese and stir until melted. Add salt and pepper to taste. Drizzle a small amount of sauce into beaten egg yolks. Slowly combine egg yolk mixture with remaining sauce. Add mushrooms and remaining seafood.

Pour into individual casseroles or one large dish. Cover with bread crumbs and sprinkle with more cheese and paprika, if desired. Bake at 350 degrees for 25-30 minutes, or until heated through and crumbs are brown.

May be prepared early in the day and refrigerated. Bring casserole to room temperature and bake as directed.

Serve with green salad and your favorite chardonnay.

Number of Servings: 10-12

Teriyaki Flank Steak

2 pounds flank steak

$^1/_2$ cup teriyaki sauce or
   a mixture of teriyaki
   and soy sauce
1 clove garlic, crushed
1 bay leaf
$^1/_4$ cup oil (vegetable or
   olive, amount may be
   reduced)
2 tablespoons balsamic
   vinegar
1 teaspoon dry mustard
   Black pepper

Combine ingredients (except pepper) in a plastic bag.
Marinate steak for at least 3-4 hours, or overnight.
Season steaks with black pepper just before you grill
or broil. They don't need salt due to the soy sauce.

Grill or broil 8 minutes per side for rare; 10 minutes
per side for medium rare. Check halfway through
cooking time, as broilers and grill heat varies. Let
steak set for 5-10 minutes after removing from heat
source.

Slice steak thinly against the grain and serve.

This is delicious served warm or cold. Can be served
with meal or used in fajitas and salads.

Number of Servings: 4

Bulgur Pilaf with Peppers and Tomato

The perfect side dish.

4 tablespoons unsalted butter

1 large Spanish onion, diced (1 cup)

1 small Italian green pepper, finely chopped ($^1/_4$ cup)

1 small red bell pepper, finely chopped ($^1/_4$ cup)

1$^1/_2$ cups coarse-grain bulgur, washed and drained

3 medium tomatoes, peeled, seeded, and finely chopped (2 cups)

2$^1/_2$ teaspoons ground red pepper

2$^1/_2$ cups chicken stock or hot water

Salt and freshly ground black pepper

2 tablespoons fresh Italian parsley, coarsely chopped

In a heavy, medium-sized saucepan, heat the butter over medium heat and cook the onion gently for 2 minutes, stirring with a wooden spoon until it's softened but not brown. Stir in the green pepper, red bell pepper, bulgur, tomatoes, ground red pepper, and stock. Season with salt and pepper. Bring the mixture to a boil, then lower the heat, cover the saucepan, and cook gently for about 15 minutes, or until the bulgur has absorbed all the liquid. Let the mixture stand, covered, for about 5 minutes. Stir in the parsley and serve.

Number of Servings: 4-6

Taco Pie

Kids really like this—can be made in the morning and baked later.

1 pound ground beef
  (or turkey)
1 medium onion, chopped
1 deep dish pie shell
1 package taco seasoning
1 can refried beans
1 (8 ounce) jar taco sauce
2 cups cheddar cheese
12 nacho chips
   Shredded lettuce
   Chopped tomatoes

Preheat oven to 400 degrees. Prick pie shell and bake for 10 minutes. Reduce oven temperature to 350 degrees. Brown ground beef with chopped onion. Add taco seasoning according to package directions.

In a small bowl, combine refried beans and $1/2$ cup taco sauce; mix well. Layer $1/2$ refried bean mixture in bottom of pie shell. Top with $1/2$ the meat mixture, add 1 cup shredded cheese and nacho chips. Repeat layers but omit the nacho chips. Bake at 350 degrees, 20-30 minutes. Remove from oven, top with lettuce and tomatoes. Serve with the rest of the taco sauce.

Note:
Ground turkey and low fat cheddar will reduce fat and tastes very good.

Number of Servings: 8

About the Filene Center:

In 1991, Garrison Keillor's NPR radio hit about the news from the fictional town of Lake Wobegon, *A Prairie Home Companion*, was broadcast live from the Filene Center stage for the first time and continues to be one of the summer season's hottest tickets.

Sautéed Escargot with Provincale Herbs, Ginger Shortbread, and Tamarind Jus

Chef's Best Recipe

Vikram Garg - Executive Chef

Indebleu
707 G Street, NW
Washington, DC

Ginger shortbread:
- 5 ounces flour
- 2 ounces butter
- Pinch salt
- 1 ounce water
- 1 ounce candied ginger

Escargot:
- 4 garlic cloves, peeled
- 16 pearl onions, peeled
- 1 (18 count) can escargot
- 8 cherry tomatoes
- 1-2 sprigs fresh rosemary
- 1 sprig fresh thyme
- 1 sprig fresh oregano
- 1 sprig fresh marjoram
  (1 tablespoon of dried Herbs de Provence may be substituted for the fresh herbs)

For ginger shortbread:
Sift flour with salt, rub flour and soft butter between your palms. Add water and finely chopped candied ginger and knead. Roll out $1/8$ inch thick and cut into $1/4$ x 6 inch long strips. Bake at 325 degrees for 18-20 minutes or until light brown. Remove and set aside to cool.

For escargot:
Chop all herbs fine (for dried herbs leave as is). Heat olive oil in an 8 inch pan, add garlic and pearl onions and sauté until light brown. Add escargot, cherry tomatoes, chopped herbs and sauté until mixture is hot. Pour in tamarind jus and bring to a boil.

For tamarind jus:
Mix all the ingredients in a saucepan and bring to boil. Reduce heat and let simmer until reduced by half.

(continued on next page)

108

Sautéed Escargot with Provincale Herbs, Ginger Shortbread, and Tamarind Jus

Tamarind jus:
    5 ounces duck and veal
        demi glaze (available
        frozen from specialty
        shops)
    1 sprig rosemary
    1 sprig thyme
        A few red chili flakes
    3 ounces natural tamarind
        extract
    1 teaspoon honey
    1/8 teaspoon crushed
        black pepper
        Salt to taste
    4 leaves basil
    8 leaves parsley
    2 ounces virgin olive oil

Garnish:
    1 ounce candied ginger,
        thinly sliced

To serve:
Divide escargot mixture in four deep plates. Pour the remaining sauce over it. Place the ginger shortbread on top. Garnish with candied ginger and chopped parsley. Serve hot.

Note:
Shrimp can be substituted for escargot.

Number of Servings: 6

Chilies and Cheese

This simple, quick dish is a crowd pleaser. Serve for breakfast, lunch, or dinner, as an appetizer or side dish.

**36 ounces shredded
    jack cheese
  4 (4 ounce) cans green
    chilies, chopped
  8 eggs, beaten**

Grease 9x13 inch glass baking dish. Layer cheese and chilies in dish twice ($\frac{1}{2}$ and $\frac{1}{2}$). Beat eggs and pour over cheese and chilies. Bake at 300 degrees for 45 minutes, until center is firm.

May be served hot, warm, or cool. Cut into larger squares for meal portion or into small squares as a tasty appetizer.

Number of Servings: 6-8

About the Filene Center:

Wolf Trap once provided a Composer's Cottage that was a tranquil residence for the creation of new works. Aaron Copland, Stanley Hollingsworth, Earl Wild, and Elie Siegmeister created works there before it was destroyed by fire in 1979.

Fusilli Pasta with Bacon and Figs

½ pound fusilli pasta
2 tablespoons olive oil
4-6 ounces smoked
    bacon, cut into
    ½ inch dice
2 small onions, cut into
    ½ inch dice
    About 9 fresh figs,
    quartered
1 tablespoon fresh parsley,
    chopped
6 slices prosciutto,
    chopped
    Salt and pepper to taste

Bring a large pot of salted water to a boil. Add the pasta and cook according to package directions.

Meanwhile, heat the oil in a large skillet over medium-high heat. Add the bacon or pancetta and onion and cook, stirring occasionally, until the bacon is crisp and the onion is softened, 10-15 minutes. If desired, drain some of the drippings from the skillet. Add the figs and cook, stirring frequently, for 2 minutes. Remove the skillet from the heat; set aside.

Drain the pasta. Transfer it to the serving dish, add the bacon mixture and toss to combine. If desired, add the prosciutto and additional oil and salt to taste. Toss to combine. Top with chopped parsley and serve immediately.

Number of Servings: 2

Party Paella

6 tablespoons olive oil
1 pound chorizo or hot
  Italian sausage, cut into
  1 inch pieces
3½ pounds chicken
  breasts, boned and cut
  into serving size pieces
2½ pounds large shrimp,
  shelled and deveined
8 bacon slices, cooked and
  chopped
2 green peppers, coarsely
  chopped
2 onions, chopped
2 cloves garlic, minced
3 tomatoes, skinned and
  quartered
1 (8 ounce) jar pimentos,
  chopped
3 teaspoons paprika
¼ teaspoon saffron
2 bay leaves, crumbled
5 tablespoons parsley,
  chopped
2 cups uncooked long
  grain rice
3½ cups chicken broth
1 teaspoon lemon juice
½ cup dry white wine
  Salt and pepper to taste
1 cup frozen green peas,
  thawed
2 lemons, sliced in wedges

In 10-14 inch paella pan or large heavy oven-proof skillet, heat oil. Sauté chorizo over medium heat 5 minutes. Add chicken. Cook additional 5 minutes, stirring, until chicken is golden. Remove chicken and sausage to warm bowl. Add shrimp to pan. Sauté 3 minutes or until shrimp is barely pink. Remove to warm bowl. Add crumbled bacon.

Add peppers, onion, and garlic to the pan. Sauté until golden, 2-3 minutes. Stir in tomatoes and pimento. Cook 10 minutes over low heat. Add paprika, saffron, parsley, bay leaf, and rice. Stir to coat rice well with oil.

Bring chicken broth to low boil. Add to rice mixture. Stir. Add lemon juice, wine, salt, and pepper. Stir in peas. Bring to boil over medium heat. Cook uncovered 6-8 minutes, stirring occasionally.

Add chicken, sausage, and shrimp. Bake uncovered in preheated 325 degree oven for 15 minutes. More broth may be added if mixture seems too dry. Remove from oven and cover lightly. Let stand for 10 minutes before serving.

Serve with lemon wedge.

Number of Servings: 8-10

Jammin' Jambalaya

A Fat Tuesday feast for anytime of the year.

3 pounds boneless chicken breasts, cut into serving size pieces
3-4 tablespoons bacon drippings or butter, divided
2 large onions, chopped
1 red bell pepper, diced
1 green pepper, diced
1 clove garlic, minced
2 tablespoons flour
1 pound smoked sausage, sliced
4 celery stalks, diced
$1/2$ teaspoon ground black pepper
3 cups tomatoes, peeled, seeded, and chopped
$1/2$ teaspoon thyme
$1/2$ teaspoon hot sauce
1 cup water
1 cup tomato juice
$3/4$ cup uncooked rice
$1/2$ pound cooked jumbo shrimp, shelled and deveined
2 small cooked lobster tails, shelled and quartered
$1/2$ cup scallions, thinly sliced
2 bay leaves
$1/2$ cup parsley

Season chicken with salt and pepper. Sauté in 2 tablespoons bacon drippings or butter. Remove chicken from pan.

In same skillet sauté onions, green pepper, red bell pepper, and garlic. Remove from skillet. Add remaining drippings or butter and flour. Stirring often, simmer until light brown.

Stir in sausage, chicken, onions, celery, pepper, garlic, and 2 cups tomatoes. Stirring constantly, cook 10 minutes. Add thyme, $1/2$ teaspoon pepper, hot sauce, water, tomato juice, and rice. Mix well. Bring to boil. Reduce heat and cover. Simmer 30 minutes. Stir in shrimp, lobster, scallions, bay leaves, remaining 1 cup tomatoes, and parsley. Cook 5 minutes. Remove bay leaves before serving.

Serve in large bowls. Garnish with chopped parsley.

Number of Servings: 10-12

114

Roasted Duckling with Honey Orange Sauce

¼ cup shallots, chopped
½ teaspoon ground ginger
3 cloves garlic, crushed
4 tablespoons soy sauce
2 (5-7 pound) ducks, quartered

Orange sauce:
½ cup orange juice
4 oranges, peeled and sectioned
4 tablespoons cooking wine
4 tablespoons sugar
3 tablespoons honey
4 tablespoons red wine vinegar
1 cup beef or chicken stock
2 teaspoons cornstarch
2 tablespoons cold water

Combine shallots, ginger, garlic, and soy sauce. Mix well. Rub duck generously with mixture. Let stand at room temperature 1-2 hours. Place on rack in baking pan. Roast in preheated 300 degree oven 3 hours or until crisp.

Peel orange sections, reserving juice. Combine orange sections with orange juice and wine. Let stand at room temperature. In heavy large saucepan combine sugar, honey, and vinegar. Cook uncovered over high heat until caramelized, about 2-3 minutes. Stir in stock immediately.

Skim off fat from duck pan juices. Add pan juices and drained juice from orange sections to caramelized stock. Combine 2 teaspoons cornstarch with 2 tablespoons cold water. Add to saucepan. Cook over medium heat until thickened and bubbly, stirring constantly. Stir in orange sections. Spoon over duck sections and serve immediately.

Number of Servings: 6-8

About the Filene Center:

The Filene Center was named after Wolf Trap Founder Catherine Filene Shouse's parents.

Corn Spoon Bread

Former First Lady Barbara Bush

President and Mrs. Bush have many favorite dishes, but this recipe is one of the family's most popular dishes.

3 eggs
$^1/_3$ cup oil
1 (10 ounce) can creamed corn
1 cup yellow corn meal
$^3/_4$ cup milk
1 teaspoon salt
4 ounces chopped green chilies (available in 4.25 ounce can) (optional)
1 cup cheddar cheese, grated

Beat eggs and oil in mixing bowl and add all remaining ingredients. Lightly grease 3 inch deep by 12 inch baking dish and bake in 375 degree oven for 35-45 minutes.

(If you double the recipe, cook for 45-50 minutes)

Number of Servings: 6

Eggplant Soufflé

1 medium-large eggplant
2 tablespoons butter
2 small cloves garlic,
  finely minced
2 tablespoons flour
1 cup milk, warmed
3 egg yolks, lightly beaten
2-3 ounces Parmesan or
  Romano cheese, grated
1/2 teaspoon freshly
  ground pepper
4 egg whites
1/4 cup fresh parsley,
  chopped

Bake eggplant in preheated 350 degree oven 50 minutes or until thoroughly cooked. When cool, slice in half. Drain well. Scrape pulp and mash well. Discard skin.

In large saucepan melt butter and add garlic. Stir in flour. Cook slowly 2-3 minutes. Stirring constantly, add milk and cook until mixture thickens. Remove from heat. Blend in egg yolks, cheese, pepper, and eggplant.

Beat egg whites until stiff but not dry. Add egg whites to eggplant mixture. Fold in gently. Pour mixture into 6-cup soufflé dish. Bake in preheated 350 degree oven 45-50 minutes. Garnish with chopped parsley and serve immediately.

Number of Servings: 6

About the Filene Center:

In April 1982, a devastating fire burned the Filene Center completely to the ground. The cause of the fire is unknown. Friends and supporters of Wolf Trap worked together to overcome this tragedy and the Filene Center was rebuilt and opened again in 1984. In the meantime, a temporary structure, the Meadow Center, was erected for the 1982 and 1983 seasons. Performances proceeded as scheduled in the temporary structure with only one canceled performance.

Fried Rice with Shrimp

4 tablespoons vegetable oil, divided

2 eggs, beaten

1 small green pepper, diced

1 small yellow onion, diced

3 pounds shrimp, shelled and deveined

1 cup frozen green peas, thawed

3 whole scallions, chopped

5 cups cooked white rice, cooled

$^1/_2$ teaspoon salt

4 tablespoons soy sauce
   Ground pepper to taste

In large skillet heat 2 tablespoons oil. Scramble eggs and transfer to plate. In same skillet sauté green pepper and onion until soft. Add shrimp, peas, and scallions, sauté 1-2 minutes or until shrimp turn pink. Remove to plate with eggs. Add remaining 2 tablespoons oil to pan. Blend in rice and cook over medium-low heat 5 minutes, stirring often. Add eggs and shrimp mixture to rice. Stir together over medium heat. Sprinkle with salt and soy sauce. Toss and serve.

Number of Servings: 6-8

Mrs. Shouse's Burgoo

Catherine Filene Shouse, Wolf Trap Founder

A Kentucky specialty often served at Wolf Trap in the early years.

To serve 20 people:
- ½ cup olive oil
- 5 pounds lean stew meat
- 3 pounds stewing chickens
- 8 pounds potatoes
- 1½ quarts canned tomatoes
- 1 pint tomato purée
- 2 pounds onions, peeled
- 1 pound cabbage, shredded
- 2 (15 ounce) cans corn
- 1 (15 ounce) can carrots
- ½ squirrel, skinned and cleaned
- ¼ bottle Worcestershire sauce
- Salt and pepper to taste

To serve 2000 people:
- 1 quart olive oil
- 250 pounds lean stew meat
- 120 pounds stewing chickens
- 400 pounds potatoes
- 18 gallons canned tomatoes
- 3 gallons tomato purée
- 100 pounds onions, peeled
- 50 pounds cabbage, shredded
- 24 (15 ounce) cans corn
- 3 (1 gallon) cans carrots
- 24 squirrels, skinned and cleaned
- 12½ bottles Worcestershire sauce
- Salt and pepper to taste

Heat olive oil in large stock pot. Add meat and chicken and cook for 3 hours on very low heat. Add other ingredients and cook for 8 hours on very low heat.

HINT: This recipe is best made 2-3 days ahead and kept simmering until ready to serve.

Number of Servings: 20-2000

119

Arch's Favorite Mashed Potatoes

Arch Campbell - Entertainment Reporter

These mashed potatoes are zesty and tasty and remind me of my hometown of San Antonio, Texas. About once a month we have them for dinner – and nothing else!

20 small red potatoes
1 can tomatoes with chilies
8 ounces low fat sour cream
½ cup 2% fat shredded cheddar cheese

Preheat oven to 350 degrees. Cook potatoes in boiling water until tender. Drain. In food processor, blend potatoes, tomatoes, and sour cream until smooth. Place potato mixture into a 2 quart baking dish. Bake for 25-30 minutes, until bubbly hot. Sprinkle with cheese and bake until the cheese melts. Can serve as a side dish or as a main dish.

Number of Servings: 6

Lamb and Pork Stew in a Pumpkin Shell

5 tablespoons butter
2 1/2 pounds lamb
(from the leg), cut into
1/2 inch cubes
1 pound pork cut into
1 inch cubes
2 cups onions, coarsely
chopped
2 tablespoons sugar
1 (13 ounce) can chicken
broth
2 teaspoons salt
1/2 teaspoon fresh ground
pepper
8 pound pumpkin
32 medium dried apricot
halves
1 box frozen okra,
thawed and trimmed
1 (20 ounce) can
cannelloni (white
kidney beans), drained
and rinsed
1 cup walnuts, roughly
chopped
2 tablespoons dill, snipped

Heat butter in heavy pan with lid. Brown lamb in several batches. Set aside, and brown pork. Set aside.

Add onions and cook until wilted, about 3 minutes. Add sugar and allow it to caramelize in pan for a few minutes. Add broth and bring to a simmer. Add salt and pepper. Add meats and their juices. Bring to a simmer, cover, and cook for 30 minutes. The stew can be chilled at this point.

Preheat oven to 350 degrees about 1 1/2 hours before dinner.

Cut the lid from pumpkin and clean out seeds and membrane. Replace lid and bake pumpkin for 1 hour on a pan.

About 25 minutes before dinner bring stew to a simmer. Add apricots and simmer for 10 minutes. Add okra and simmer, covered, for 5 additional minutes. Add beans and walnuts and simmer for 5 minutes more.

To serve:
Take pumpkin from oven and remove the lid. Ladle stew into it and sprinkle on dill. When serving, be sure to scrape some of the pumpkin onto each serving.

Number of Servings: 8-10

Mesquite Barbecued Salmon

1 cup mesquite or hickory wood chips
  Vegetable oil for grill
1 cup fresh lemon juice
1 cup vegetable oil
1 teaspoon Worcestershire sauce
2 pounds fresh salmon steaks
$1/2$ teaspoon seasoned salt
$1/2$ teaspoon fresh thyme, crumbled

Soak wood chips in water for 20 minutes.

Combine lemon juice, vegetable oil, and Worcestershire sauce. Marinate salmon in mixture at least 30 minutes.

Remove salmon from the marinade. Season with salt and thyme and let stand 15-20 minutes. Brush grill grate with cooking oil and sprinkle soaked wood chips over the hot coals. Grill fish until done, about 6-7 minutes per side for 1 inch steaks.

Hint:
For picnic use, grill ahead and chill in the refrigerator. Transport to picnic and serve cool but not ice cold.

Number of Servings: 6-8

Celebration Chicken

Oasis Winery
14141 Hume Road
Hume, VA 22639

This recipe from Virginia's own Oasis Winery is ideal for your next hospitality or entertaining opportunity.

Flour mixture:
   2 cups flour
   1/4 cup each oregano, basil, and thyme
   Salt and pepper as desired

20 (3-4 ounce) boneless, skinless chicken breasts
1/2 cup extra virgin olive oil
1/3 pound unsalted butter
8 shallots
1/2 cup fresh garlic, chopped
1 bottle Oasis Chardonnay
1 (12 ounce) can chicken stock
3 cups heavy cream
1/2 cup fresh basil, chopped
1/2 cup fresh thyme, chopped
1/2 cup fresh oregano, chopped
   Salt and pepper to taste

Combine flour, herbs, salt, and pepper. Lightly dust the chicken breasts in the flour mixture.

In a heavy sauté pan, heat 1/2 cup olive oil on low heat. Gradually add chicken and brown on each side and remove.

When chicken is browned, pour out oil and add 1/3 pound butter. Sauté 1/2 cup shallots and 1/2 cup garlic in butter until golden in color, add one bottle of Oasis Chardonnay. Reduce liquid by half and add 1 cup chicken stock and 3 cups heavy cream. Reduce until slightly thickened and add remaining basil, thyme, and oregano. Remove from heat and add salt and pepper to taste.

Preheat oven to 350 degrees. Place chicken breasts on large cookie tray or other baking dish, top with mixture and bake for 20 minutes. Serve immediately.

Number of Servings: 16-20

Sound Check Chili

A unique version of traditional Southwestern Green Chili that looks red.

4 tablespoons olive oil
2 cloves fresh garlic
1 fresh white onion, coarsely chopped
2 pounds regular (not lean) ground beef
4 tablespoons flour
2-6 tablespoons ground red chili powder
4 fresh green chilies, chopped
1 teaspoon ground cumin
½ cup fresh, or 2 tablespoons dried oregano
Salt and pepper to taste
1 large can white hominy (optional)
1 package corn tortillas
16 ounces colby cheese, coarsely grated
1 head iceberg lettuce, chopped
4 fresh tomatoes chopped
1 (12 ounce) container of sour cream

Heat 4 tablespoons olive oil in deep pan. Lightly brown 2 cloves finely chopped garlic. Add coarsely chopped white onion, and continue browning. Add hamburger. Brown until almost done. Add extra olive oil if needed.

Stir in and brown 4 tablespoons flour (consistency of ingredients should be sticky and thick) to make gravy base. Stir in and brown 2-6 tablespoons red chili powder. Raise heat and continue to stir and brown mixture for 1 minute.

Add 4 cups cold water a little at a time, until boiling begins again, stirring constantly. Add more cold water until desired consistency is obtained, again, bring to a boil. Reduce heat to a simmer. Simmer for 20 minutes, covered, stirring occasionally.

Add chopped green chilies. Spice to taste with cumin, oregano, and salt. Additional spices may be added for desired taste. Add a large can of white hominy (optional).

Serve with corn tortillas, cooked for 1 minute on top of simmering chili, then layered flat on plate with colby cheese, lettuce, tomato, and sour cream. Cover with second corn tortilla, and smother with chili. Top with a dollop of sour cream. Salsa optional.

Number of Servings: 8-10

Oasis Beef Bourguignon

Oasis Winery
14141 Hume Road
Hume, VA 22639

This dish is ideal for smaller groups of six or less. Award-winning local wines from Oasis Winery make this a savory treat.

8 ounces thick sliced bacon, diced
3 pounds beef chuck (cut into 1 inch cubes)
1 cup onions, chopped
Salt and fresh ground pepper to taste
3 tablespoons unbleached all-purpose flour
3 cups of your favorite Oasis red wine
3 cups beef stock
2 tablespoons tomato paste
1 tablespoon fresh rosemary leaves, chopped
3 carrots, peeled and cut into 1½ inch julienne strips (1½ cups)
2 cups red and white pearl onions
1 tablespoon basil
1 tablespoon garlic
1 tablespoon unsalted butter
2 tablespoons fresh parsley, chopped

Preheat oven to 350 degrees. In a flame-proof casserole or a Dutch oven, sauté the bacon until crisp. Remove with a slotted spoon and drain. Using drippings of bacon fat over medium heat, sauté beef a few pieces at a time until golden brown on all sides. Add onions, salt, pepper, and flour. Cook over high heat, stirring constantly for 5 minutes. Add Oasis Winery red wine, beef stock, tomato paste, rosemary, garlic, and basil, bring to boil. Cover casserole, transfer to the oven. Bake until the meat is tender (approximately 2 hours).

In additional pot, bring water to a boil. Drop in carrots and boil until tender. Drain and shock. Repeat for the pearl onions. Melt butter and sauté remaining garlic in a small skillet over medium heat. Set aside.

When the meat is cooked, transfer casserole to burner and add carrots and onions. Heat through for 7 minutes. Serve garnished with chopped parsley.

Number of Servings: 6

FUNCTIONAL TOUCHES *can* *add* CONVENIENCE *to your kitchen.*

With busy schedules, Americans are always looking for simple and convenient products to help make cooking and cleaning in the kitchen hassle-free.

To help you create a kitchen that's tailored to the way you live, following are some tips from Reico Kitchen & Bath, the leading supplier of kitchen and bath products and services in the Washington, D.C. area.

CONVENIENCE:

- Pull-out trays in base cabinets eliminate the hassle of stooping down and digging out items to get at the pot stored in the back.

- A cutting board kit installed inside a cabinet drawer puts knives and a cutting board in one convenient location.

- Roll-out wastebaskets and recycling bins next to the kitchen sink help make cleaning a snap while keeping the receptacles out of sight.

- A tilt-out sink tray installed on the front of the kitchen sink keeps sponges and scrubbers handy for quick clean-up.

- A warming drawer built underneath the countertop allows bread to keep warm until served.

More Function and Innovation tips from Reico can be found throughout the book.

Blueberry Sour Cream Pie

The best of the best! The leftovers are even better the following day, especially right out of the refrigerator. Also terrific served with vanilla ice cream or frozen yogurt.

Pie:
- 9 inch pie shell
- 3/4 cup sugar
- 3 tablespoons flour
- 1 large egg
- 1 3/4 cups sour cream
- 2 teaspoons cinnamon
- 1/2 teaspoon nutmeg
- 2 teaspoons vanilla extract
- 1/2 teaspoon lemon rind, grated
- 3 cups blueberries, washed and dried

Topping:
- 1/2 cup sugar
- 1/2 cup brown sugar
- 1/2 cup flour
- 2 teaspoons cinnamon
- 1/4 pound unsalted butter, very cold
- 1/2 cup walnuts, chopped

Prepare 9 inch unbaked pie shell. Combine ingredients for pie and put into the pie shell, mounding in the middle. Bake at 350 degrees for 30 minutes.

Combine first four ingredients for topping. Cut in butter. Mix with walnuts. Sprinkle mixture over the top of the pie and bake for 10-15 additional minutes.

Number of Servings: 8

About Wolf Trap Education:

Wolf Trap Education's largest program is the Wolf Trap Institute for Early Learning Through the Arts. This program provides artist residencies in preschool classrooms and works with teachers to incorporate arts-based teaching strategies to engage children and build a foundation for future learning.

Chocolate Chip Cookies

Marvin Hamlisch, Composer/Conductor

I really think these are the best chocolate chip cookies I've ever had. And because my mother-in-law makes them, they're FREE!!!

$2^1/4$ cups and 1 teaspoon all-purpose flour
1 teaspoon baking soda
$^1/2$ teaspoon salt
1 cup (2 sticks) butter, softened
$^3/4$ cup granulated sugar
2 eggs
1 teaspoon vanilla extract
2 cups (12 ounce package) semi-sweet chocolate morsels

Preheat oven to 375 degrees.

Combine flour, baking soda and salt in a small bowl. Mix together butter and sugar. Beat in eggs, one at a time, and vanilla. Gradually beat in flour mixture. Stir in morsels.

Drop by rounded teaspoon onto ungreased baking sheets. Bake 9-11 minutes. Do not over bake. Let stand for 2 minutes. Remove to wire racks to cool.

Number of Servings: Makes about 5 dozen.

Fresh Apple Cake

This apple cake is made from scratch and has a wonderful moist flavor.

2 cups sugar
1½ cups cooking oil
2 teaspoons vanilla
3 small eggs, well beaten
3 tablespoons fresh
   lemon juice
1 teaspoon salt
3 cups unbleached flour
2 teaspoons cinnamon
2 teaspoons nutmeg
1½ teaspoons baking soda
4 large Granny Smith
   apples, peeled, cored, and
   chopped

Brown Sugar Glaze:
1 stick unsalted butter
1 cup brown sugar
⅓ cup milk

Combine and beat well the first 5 ingredients. Sift together the salt, flour, cinnamon, nutmeg, and baking soda and add to the above mixture. Add the 4 peeled and chopped apples to mixture. Mixture will be stiff, so you may need to mix with your hands. Bake in greased and floured tube pan for 1½ hours at 325 degrees.

While the cake is baking, make the glaze. Brush on cake, once slightly cooled and removed from pan.

Brown Sugar Glaze:
Melt butter in pan and add brown sugar and milk. Bring to a boil and boil for 3 minutes, stirring continuously. Cool slightly. Punch holes all over cake with ice pick and brush warm glaze over the entire cake. Save some of the glaze to dribble over each slice on the plate before serving. Make sure the glaze is warm.

Before serving, put a few raspberries, blueberries, and/or sliced strawberries on each plate to add color. Delicious with cinnamon or vanilla ice cream.

Number of Servings: 8-10

Lemon Layer Cake

Cake:

- 2½ cups cake flour
- 2 teaspoons baking powder
- ½ teaspoon baking soda
- ¼ teaspoon salt
- 1 cup unsalted butter, softened
- 1½ cups granulated sugar
- 2 whole eggs
- 3 egg yolks
- 3 teaspoons vanilla extract
- 1 teaspoon lemon zest
- ½ cup fresh lemon juice
- ½ cup whole milk

Lemon filling:

- 2 egg yolks
- ⅓ cup granulated sugar
- ¼ cup fresh lemon juice
- 2 tablespoons unsalted butter, softened
- 2 teaspoons lemon zest
- ½ cup heavy cream

Lemon frosting:

- ¾ cup unsalted butter, softened
- 3½ cups powdered sugar
- 2 tablespoons heavy cream
- 2 teaspoons fresh lemon juice
- ¼ teaspoon vanilla extract
- 1 teaspoon lemon zest
- 1 cup roasted blanched almonds, finely chopped (Roast in oven for 5-10 minutes or until almonds turn slightly brown. Let cool completely and chop in food processor.)

Preheat oven to 350 degrees. Butter and flour bottom and sides of two 9 inch round cake tins.

In a mixing bowl sift together flour, baking powder, baking soda, and salt. In separate mixing bowl beat the butter on medium speed until creamy, about 30-45 seconds. Slowly add sugar and mix until light and smooth. Add whole eggs and egg yolks. Add vanilla and lemon zest. Slowly add lemon juice. The mixture will appear curdled until you add dry ingredients.

Combine dry ingredients, butter mixture, and milk. Beat slowly and mix well. Pour batter into prepared pans. Bake for 20-25 minutes or until a toothpick comes clean after inserting it in the middle of the cake. Cool cakes upside down on cooling racks for 40 minutes.

Lemon filling:
In a small sauce pan, whisk yolks and sugar until combined. Add lemon juice and butter. Cook over medium low heat, stirring constantly with a wooden spoon until mixture thickens. Do not let mixture come to a boil; it will curdle. Strain mixture through a fine sieve into another glass bowl. Add lemon zest and let the mixture cool. Cover and refrigerate until chilled. In a clean bowl whip heavy cream until soft peaks form. Fold whipped cream into the chilled filling. Cover and refrigerate until ready to assemble.

Lemon frosting:
In a large bowl beat butter until creamy. Beat in powdered sugar until smooth. Add heavy cream, lemon juice, vanilla, and lemon zest. Continue beating until mixture is light and airy.

To assemble cake, spread lemon filling evenly onto first layer with a spatula. Leave about one inch space from the edge of the cake. Place second layer on top. Frost top and sides of the cake with frosting. Slightly tilt cake on an angle and drizzle chopped almonds onto the side of the cake.

Number of Servings: 12

Dick's Favorite Ice Cream

Dick Smothers - Folk Musician and Comedian

I'm an ice cream fanatic. This is quick and easy and doesn't need an ice cream maker.

Juice of 3 lemons
1½ cups sugar
4 cups heavy cream
1 tablespoon lemon zest (grated lemon rind)
Raspberries
Strawberries
Mint sprigs

Dissolve sugar in lemon juice. Add cream and stir. Stir in lemon zest. Freeze until solid. Rewhip and refreeze. Garnish with fresh raspberries, strawberries, and mint sprigs.

Number of Servings: 8

About Wolf Trap Education:

Wolf Trap's Education programs include Children's Theatre-in-the-Woods, an outdoor performance venue that hosts 70 performances each summer featuring storytellers, puppetry, music, dance, and theater.

Apricot Bars

This is a good Charleston, South Carolina recipe.

1 cup butter
1 cup granulated sugar
2 egg yolks
2 cups flour, not sifted
1 teaspoon vanilla
1 teaspoon lemon zest
1 (12 ounce) jar apricot
preserves

Cream butter and sugar. Add beaten egg yolks. Fold in flour, vanilla, and zest. Pat dough into 2 balls the size of oranges. Chill for 2 hours. In 9x13 inch baking pan, pat one ball of dough flat in the pan. Spread the apricot preserves over the top. Slice the other ball of dough into $1/8$ inch rounds and place over the preserves. Bake at 350 degrees for 35 minutes, or until the bars start to get brown around the edge.

Number of Servings: 48

About Wolf Trap Education:

The stART smART Network, a distance learning program developed by Wolf Trap, is an online community for early childhood educators that features arts-based teaching strategies.

Lemon Squares

Mollie Parnis Livingston and Mrs. Lyndon B. Johnson

Mollie Parnis Livingston, a dear friend of Mrs. Johnson's, gave her this recipe for lemon squares, and it is one of her favorites. The cook at the LBJ ranch keeps them in the freezer so Mrs. Johnson will always have them when she wants a snack or a delicious ending to a meal!

Crust:
- 2 cups flour
- 1/4 cup sugar
- 1 cup butter (unsalted)

Filling:
- 3 eggs
- 2 lemons
- 2 cups sugar
- 1 teaspoon baking powder
- 4 tablespoons flour

Crust:
Mix flour and sugar together. Add cold butter cut into cubes. Continue to cut the butter into the flour/sugar mixture with a pastry cutter until butter resembles pea-shaped balls. Pat mixture into a rectangular 9x13 inch baking dish (glass or aluminum).

Bake crust for 15-25 minutes at 350 degrees until very light brown.

Filling:
Beat 3 eggs in a small bowl and set aside. Zest the rind of two lemons and chop finely. Squeeze the juice from those lemons and remove all seeds. Mix 2 cups sugar, 1 teaspoon baking powder, 4 tablespoons flour, 3 beaten whole eggs, lemon zest, and lemon juice. Mix with whisk. Pour over the baked crust and bake at 350 degrees for 12-15 minutes or until set.

Remove from oven and cool. Sprinkle with powdered sugar and cut into squares.

Number of Servings: 24-30 small squares

Coconut Rice Pudding

Just delicious!

1 cup arborio rice
1 cup milk
1 (14 ounce) can coconut
   milk
2 cups cream
1 vanilla bean, scraped
1/2 cup golden raisins
1 teaspoon vanilla extract
1 large egg
1 cup cream
1/4 cup honey or
   maple syrup

Combine rice, milk, coconut milk, cream, vanilla bean, raisins, and vanilla extract in saucepan and cook on lowest possible heat until it simmers. Simmer approximately 25 minutes, stirring occasionally. Add egg and cook, stirring for a minute. Take off heat and pour into shallow dish and allow mixture to cool. Whip cream and honey (or maple syrup) and fold into cooled rice mixture.

Number of Servings: 6-8

About Wolf Trap Education:

The Center for Education at Wolf Trap is the head-quarters for the Wolf Trap Foundation for the Performing Arts located in Vienna, Virginia. This national arts and education center is equipped with a multimedia research and learning center, distance learning technology, and a 100-seat lecture hall.

B.B.'s German Chocolate Double Delight

B.B. King - Blues Performer

I claim both Indianola, Mississippi and Memphis, Tennessee as my home. I was born on a plantation in Indianola and my career was launched in Memphis. Both places are rich in music heritage and famous for their down-home cooking.

4 ounces German sweet
   chocolate
1/2 cup boiling water
1 cup butter
2 cups sugar
4 egg yolks, unbeaten
1 teaspoon vanilla
2 1/2 cups cake flour
1/2 teaspoon salt
1 teaspoon baking soda
1 cup buttermilk
4 egg whites, stiffly beaten

Coconut Pecan Frosting:
1 cup evaporated milk
1 cup sugar
3 egg yolks
1/2 cup butter or margarine
1 teaspoon vanilla
1 1/3 cups coconut, shredded
1 cup pecans, chopped

Melt chocolate above boiling water in a double boiler and let cool. Cream the butter and sugar in a mixing bowl until fluffy. Add egg yolks, one at a time, and beat well after each addition. Add the melted chocolate and vanilla; mix well. Sift flour, salt, and baking soda and add alternately with buttermilk to chocolate mixture, beating until smooth after each addition. Fold in the beaten egg whites. Pour into three 8-9 inch layer pans lined with paper and bake at 350 degrees for 30-40 minutes. Cool and frost only middle and top with coconut-pecan frosting.

Frosting:
In saucepan, combine milk, sugar, egg yolks, butter, and vanilla. Cook over medium heat stirring constantly until thickened. Add coconut and pecans, and beat until thick enough to spread. (Makes 2 1/2 cups.)

Number of Servings: 8

Elevator Spice Cookies

The cookies are soft and nearly a perfect circle. They are fun to bake because one does, in fact, bang the cookie sheet as the cookies come out of the oven to make them "fall." Catherine Filene Shouse was a big fan of these cookies.

½ cup butter (melted)
1 cup sugar
¼ cup molasses
1 unbeaten egg
2 cups flour
2 teaspoons baking soda
¼ teaspoon salt
1 teaspoon cinnamon
½ teaspoon cloves
½ teaspoon ginger

Combine the first four ingredients and set aside. Stir together the remaining ingredients. Add butter mixture to flour mixture and mix well. Form large walnut size balls, rolling smooth between hands. Place on greased cookie sheet, widely spaced. Bake at 350 degrees for 6-8 minutes. They should puff up like little igloos with cracked tops. Remove from oven and bang cookie sheet on top of stove so that cookies flatten out. Cool briefly on cookie sheet and then remove to racks. Cookies will hold up well in a sealed container or plastic bag.

Number of Servings: 50 cookies

About Wolf Trap Education:

Wolf Trap anticipates that the impact of its education programs will be felt by more than 16 million children, teachers, and adults over the next 20 years.

Brownies

Trisha Yearwood - Country Music Performer

These brownies do not need frosting as they develop a wonderful crunchy crust as they bake. They keep well if there are ever any left. They are a band favorite!

4 (1 ounce) squares unsweetened chocolate
$^2/_3$ cup solid shortening
2 cups sugar
4 eggs, well-beaten
1$^1/_3$ cups plain flour
1 teaspoon baking powder
1 teaspoon salt
2 cups pecans, chopped
2 teaspoons vanilla extract

Melt chocolate and shortening together in a small pan. Combine the sugar with well-beaten eggs; add the chocolate/ shortening mixture to the sugar/egg mixture. Sift flour; measure; add baking powder and salt; sift again. Add the dry ingredients to the egg mixture; add nuts and vanilla. Spread the dough evenly in a greased 9x13 pan. Bake in a moderate oven (350 degrees) 25-30 minutes. When cool, cut into squares or bars.

Number of Servings: 12 plus

About Wolf Trap Education:

Wolf Trap's Master Class series offers community members the opportunity to participate in and observe classes taught by master performing artists.

Coca-Cola Cake

This cake is great for picnics!

¼ cup cocoa
½ cup vegetable oil
1 stick butter
1 cup Coca-Cola
1½ cups mini marshmallows
3 cups flour
2 cups sugar
2 eggs
1 teaspoon baking soda
½ cup buttermilk
1 teaspoon vanilla

Icing:
1 stick butter
1 teaspoon vanilla
¼ cup cocoa
7 tablespoons Coca-Cola
1 pound box powdered
   sugar

Cake:
Mix cocoa, vegetable oil, butter, and Coca-Cola in saucepan and bring to a boil. Remove from heat. Add marshmallows and stir until melted. Set aside.

Combine flour, sugar, eggs, soda, buttermilk, and vanilla. Add to chocolate mixture. Bake 45 minutes at 325 degrees in a greased 9x13 inch pan. Ice cake while HOT!

Icing:
Make icing while the cake is baking. Combine butter, vanilla, cocoa, and Coca-Cola in pan and bring to a boil. Remove from heat and cool. Add powdered sugar. Spread on hot cake.

Refrigerate leftovers.

Number of Servings: 12-15

About Wolf Trap Education:

Master Classes have been taught by the casts of *West Side Story* and *RENT*, and by members of the Kirov Ballet and Pittsburgh Ballet Theatre. Master artists such as Boston Pops conductor, Keith Lockhart, and Placido Domingo have also led classes as part of this exciting series.

Retro Sugar Cookies

1 cup margarine, softened
1 cup powdered sugar
1 cup sugar
2 eggs (add one at a time)
1 cup vegetable oil
2 teaspoons vanilla
4½ cups flour
1 teaspoon baking soda
1 teaspoon cream of tartar
1 teaspoon salt

Mix ingredients in order. Refrigerate at least two hours or overnight. Preheat oven to 350 degrees.

Roll dough into small balls and roll them in white sugar. Place on cold, lightly greased cookie sheet and flatten with fork. Bake 10-15 minutes. Cookies can be decorated.

Number of Servings: 4-5 dozen

About Wolf Trap Education:

"The Wolf Trap Institute's programs serve hundreds of early childhood educators, parents, and caregivers by providing them with the necessary tools to develop children's basic learning skills. I am proud that the 34th District is home to such a valuable education resource as the Wolf Trap Institute." –*Vincent F. Callahan, Jr.* (Member, Virginia House of Delegates)

Chocolate Picnic Cake

This is a favorite for chocolate lovers! Freeze the cake and take on beach or mountain trips! Delicious!

2 cups flour
2 cups sugar
1/4 teaspoon salt
2 sticks margarine
4 tablespoons cocoa
1 cup water
2 eggs
1/2 cup buttermilk
1 teaspoon baking soda
1 teaspoon vanilla

Icing:
1 stick butter
4 tablespoons cocoa
6 tablespoons milk
1 box powdered sugar
1 cup pecans
1 teaspoon vanilla
Pinch of salt

Mix flour, sugar, and salt. Melt margarine, cocoa, and water in saucepan. Combine flour mixture and melted cocoa mixture. Add eggs, buttermilk, baking soda, and vanilla to mixture. Mix well and pour into an 11x14 inch pan. Bake for 20 minutes at 400 degrees.

Icing:
Boil butter, cocoa, and milk. Add powdered sugar and mix until smooth. Add pecans, salt, and vanilla and mix. Pour icing onto warm cake.

Number of Servings: 8-10

About Wolf Trap Education:

Wolf Trap offers a highly-competitive Internship Program for students across the country interested in arts administration. It is ranked by the *Princeton Review* as "One of America's Top 100 Internships."

Lemon Sorbet with Vodka-Marinated Plums

4 ripe sweet plums, pitted
  and sliced
¼ cup vodka (cassis or
  raspberry flavored,
  optional)
2 tablespoons sugar
  (or more to taste)
Lemon sorbet
  (purchased)
Fresh mint sprigs

Combine plums, vodka, and 2 tablespoons sugar in medium bowl. Taste and add more sugar if desired. Marinate at room temperature 1 hour.

Scoop sorbet into glasses. Top with plums and marinade and serve. Garnish with sprig of fresh mint.

Number of Servings: 2 (Can be doubled or tripled.)

Chocolate Cheesecake

John Eaton - Performer

This rich cheesecake is also delicious when made with a chocolate cookie crust!

9 inch crumb crust
16 ounces cream cheese
³/4 cup sugar
¹/3 cup cocoa
2 teaspoons vanilla
2 eggs
1 cup sour cream
2 tablespoons sugar
Chocolate shavings

Heat oven to 375 degrees. Make crumb crust in 9 inch springform pan. Combine cream cheese, ³/4 cup sugar, cocoa, and 1 teaspoon vanilla, mixing at medium speed on mixer until well blended. Add eggs, one at a time, mixing well after each addition. Pour mixture over crumbs. Bake for 30 minutes. Remove from oven. Cool for 15 minutes.

Increase oven temperature to 425 degrees. Combine sour cream, 2 tablespoons sugar, and remaining vanilla. Carefully spread over baked filling. Return to oven. Bake for 10 minutes. Loosen cake from rim of pan. Cool before removing rim. Chill. Garnish with chocolate shavings.

Number of Servings: 8

Strawberry Shortcake Tiramisu

2 cups ricotta cheese
1 1/2 cups cream cheese
1 1/3 cups sugar
1 teaspoon vanilla
1 pound fresh strawberries
1/2 cup orange liqueur
  (or orange juice)
36 ladyfingers, split in
  half lengthwise

Combine ricotta cheese, cream cheese, 1 cup sugar, and vanilla in food processor until smooth.

Combine half of strawberries, 1/3 cup sugar, and orange liqueur (or orange juice) in blender. Slice remaining strawberries into thin pieces.

Arrange 1/3 of ladyfinger halves in a layer of an 11x7 inch dish. Drizzle 1/3 of strawberry mixture over the ladyfingers. Spread 1/3 of ricotta cheese mixture over ladyfingers, then lay 1/3 of sliced strawberries over that. Repeat twice to create three layers.

Refrigerate for two hours before serving (or overnight if using hard ladyfingers).

Number of Servings: 12

About Wolf Trap Education:

Wolf Trap received major funding from the U.S. Department of Commerce and the National Endowment for the Arts to build the stART smART Network, an arts-based distance learning program for early childhood educators.

Peach Pie

½ cup sugar
¼ cup brown sugar
5-6 cups fresh peaches,
   sliced (approximately
   6 large peaches)
 3 tablespoons cornstarch
¼ teaspoon nutmeg
¼ teaspoon cinnamon
⅛ teaspoon salt

 1 tablespoon lemon juice
 1 tablespoon butter

 2 unbaked 9 inch pie crusts
   Butter

Combine sugars. Add to peaches and let stand 1 hour. Drain peaches, reserving juice. Combine next four ingredients in saucepan. Gradually add reserved peach juice, blending until smooth. Cook until thickened. Add sliced peaches along with lemon juice. Put into unbaked 9 inch pie crust. Dot with butter. Slice second pie crust into ½ inch strips and overlap to form lattice crust for top. Bake 10 minutes at 400 degrees, then 35 minutes at 350 degrees.

Number of Servings: 8

Key Lime Pie

Crust:
- 1½ cups finely rolled graham cracker crumbs
- ½ cup brown sugar
- ½ cup melted butter

Filling:
- 1 (14 ounce) can sweetened condensed milk
- 4 large egg yolks
- ½ cup plus 2 tablespoons fresh or bottled Key lime juice

Topping:
- ¾ cup chilled heavy cream

Crust:
Preheat oven to 325 degrees. Combine ingredients in a mixing bowl. With a fork, stir together until combined well, then press the mixture evenly on bottom and sides of a 9 inch pie plate. Place in freezer for 10 minutes. Bake crust in middle of oven 10 minutes and cool pie plate on a rack.

Filling:
Whisk condensed milk and yolks in a bowl until combined well. Add juice and whisk until combined well (mixture will thicken slightly). Pour filling into pie shell and bake in middle of oven for 15 minutes at 325 degrees. Cool pie completely on rack (filling will set as it cools) then chill covered for at least 8 hours.

Topping:
Just before serving, beat cream in a bowl with an electric mixer until it just holds stiff peaks. Serve pie topped with whipped cream. Garnish with fresh lime wheel or wedge.

Number of Servings: 6

About Wolf Trap Education:

The National Endowment for the Arts featured the Wolf Trap Institute in educational resources including *Learning Through the Arts: A Guide to the National Endowment for the Arts and Arts Education*; and *Imagine! Introducing Your Child to the Arts.*

Chocolate Fudge Sauce

Everyone's favorite ice cream topping.

1½ cups sugar
  1 stick butter
1½ cups cocoa
  3 ounces semi-sweet
    chocolate
    Pinch of salt
  1 cup whipping cream
  2 tablespoons vanilla

Combine sugar, butter, cocoa, chocolate, and salt in a saucepan. Heat until melted. Slowly add cream and vanilla. Freezes well.

Number of Servings: 8-10

About Wolf Trap Education:

The Wolf Trap Institute was awarded the 1998 Aim High Award by the Prince of Wales Trust in recognition of the program's contributions supporting the National Curriculum of Great Britain.

All-American Apple Pie

2 (9 inch) pie crusts, thawed
$1\frac{1}{4}$ cups sugar
2 tablespoons flour
$\frac{3}{4}$ teaspoon cinnamon
$\frac{1}{4}$ teaspoon nutmeg
$\frac{1}{8}$ teaspoon salt
6-7 cups thinly sliced tart green apples (about 2 pounds)
$1\frac{1}{2}$ teaspoons grated lemon peel
1 tablespoon butter

Preheat oven to 500 degrees.

In a small bowl combine sugar, flour, cinnamon, nutmeg, and salt. Mix well.

Add mixture to apples in a large bowl and combine. Turn into pastry lined pie plate, mounding apples high in the center. Sprinkle with lemon peel and dot with butter.

Cover with other pie crust. Pinch sides together. Put slits in top. Bake 8 minutes at 500 degrees. Reduce to 350 degrees and bake for 50-60 minutes.

Number of Servings: 6-8

About Wolf Trap Education:

Wolf Trap Scholarships in the Performing Arts provide local public high school teachers in the disciplines of dance, theater, and music with grants to support instruction that leads to increased student performance.

Spiced Peach Sundaes

Flavors of cardamom and nutmeg compliment these delicious sundaes.

¼ cup (½ stick) unsalted butter
6 tablespoons (packed) dark brown sugar
1 teaspoon vanilla extract
½ teaspoon ground cardamom
⅛ teaspoon ground nutmeg
2½ pounds ripe peaches, pitted, cut into ¼ inch thick slices

½ gallon vanilla ice cream
3 tablespoons peach schnapps liqueur (optional)
Whole pecans, toasted
Sweetened whipped cream

Melt butter in heavy skillet over medium heat. Add brown sugar; stir to blend. Add vanilla, cardamom, and nutmeg. Stir 1 minute. Add peaches; toss gently to coat. Cook until sugar mixture melts and peaches are tender but do not fall apart, tossing occasionally, about 5 minutes. (Can be made 8 hours ahead. Cover, chill. Rewarm over low heat before using.)

Place 2 scoops ice cream in each of 8 bowls. Spoon peach mixture over ice cream, dividing equally. Top with peach schnapps, if desired. Garnish with pecans and whipped cream.

Number of Servings: 8

About Wolf Trap Education:

Wolf Trap's renowned education programs have been featured on CBS *Sunday Morning*, NBC's *Today Show*, CNN *World News Tonight*, the BBC, C-Span, and National Public Radio; in *Southern Living* magazine, *Wall Street Journal*, *The Washington Post*, *Daily Telegraph* (London), *Financial Times* (London), and *Washington Business Journal*.

Cheddar and Pepper Biscuits

Dick Smothers - Folk Musician and Comedian

These biscuits are great with green pepper jelly.

4 cups flour
2 tablespoons baking
  powder
1/2 teaspoon salt
1/2 cup shortening
1/4 cup butter
1 1/2 cups cheddar cheese,
  shredded
3 teaspoons black pepper
1 1/2 cups milk
1 egg
1/2 teaspoon water

Preheat oven to 400 degrees.

Lightly grease a large baking sheet. Combine in a large mixing bowl the flour, baking powder, and salt. Cut in shortening and butter with a pastry blender until mixture resembles coarse crumbs. Add cheese and pepper and mix well. Make a well in the center of the dry mixture. Add milk all at once and stir until just moistened.

Turn dough out onto a lightly floured surface. Divide dough in half and roll or pat each half into a 1 inch thick cake. Cut into 2 inch squares using a sharp knife or use a 2 inch biscuit cutter. Combine egg and water and brush tops of biscuits with this mixture. Place biscuits on baking sheet and bake for 13-15 minutes or until golden. (To reheat biscuits, wrap in foil and bake at 325 degrees for 10 minutes.)

Number of Servings: 18-20 biscuits

Mormon Tabernacle Choir Christmas Fudge

Mormon Tabernacle Choir

Former Choir member, Linda Braithwaite, makes this fudge for the Choir every Christmas.

10 (8 ounce) packages
    cream cheese at room
    temperature
10 sticks butter or
    margarine at room
    temperature
  5 cups cocoa powder
20 pounds powdered
    sugar
  3 tablespoons plus
    1 teaspoon vanilla
10 cups walnuts (optional)

Single batch (3 pounds):
  1 (8 ounce) package
    cream cheese at room
    temperature
  1 stick butter or margarine
    at room temperature
$1/2$ cup cocoa powder
  2 pounds powdered sugar
  1 teaspoon vanilla
  1 cup walnuts (optional)

Combine all ingredients except walnuts. Knead with hands until all the powdered sugar is blended in. Knead in walnuts, if desired.

Press on to 9x13 inch pan or very large trays. Chill through. (Product is best if kept refrigerated.)

Number of Servings: 360 pieces (30 pounds) or 36 pieces (3 pounds) for single batch.

Creme de Menthe Brownies

Brownies:
  1 cup sugar
  ½ cup butter
  4 eggs, beaten
  1 cup flour
  ½ teaspoon salt
  1 (16 ounce) can
    chocolate syrup
  1 teaspoon vanilla

Frosting (middle layer):
  2 cups powdered sugar
  2 tablespoons white
    crème de menthe
  ½ cup butter

Glaze:
  1 cup chocolate chips
  6 tablespoons butter

Brownies:
Mix together and put batter in a greased 9x13 inch pan. Bake at 350 degrees for 30 minutes. Cool.

Frosting:
Mix and spread over cake mixture. Set aside.

Glaze:
Melt together. Let cool slightly and spread over frosting.

Chill and cut into squares.

Number of Servings: 24

About Wolf Trap Education:

The Wolf Trap Institute was included in the National Endowment for the Arts 25th anniversary book, *A Legacy of Leadership*.

Party Puffs

This is a great recipe for festive occasions. It always gets rave reviews and is so much better than cookies or cake when you have to bring a dessert.

Cream Puffs:
- ½ cup butter
- 1 cup water
- 1 cup flour
- ½ teaspoon salt
- 4 eggs

Filling:
- 2 packages (3½ ounces) instant vanilla pudding
- 2 cups heavy cream (whipping cream)
- 1 cup milk

  Powdered sugar or chocolate sauce

Cream Puffs:
In a 2 quart saucepan, bring water to boil. Add butter and melt. Add flour and salt all at once and stir until mixture leaves sides of pan. Remove from heat. Add eggs, one at a time, beating thoroughly after each addition. Drop dough by spoonfuls on baking sheet. Bake in preheated 400 degree oven for 30-35 minutes. (Use teaspoon and make about 24 half size puffs.)

Filling:
In large mixing bowl, beat ingredients until smooth and thick (2-3 minutes). Slice top off cream puffs. Spoon filling into puffs. Replace top and sprinkle with powdered sugar or drizzle with chocolate sauce.

Do not fill more then a couple of hours ahead of time as they do get soft. Refrigerate after filling.

Number of Servings: 24

Kentucky Derby Pie

Jon Anthony - Radio Personality

This is my variation of a unique, delicious dessert celebrating the biggest event each year in my home state of Kentucky!

1 stick butter, softened
1 cup sugar
2 eggs, beaten
½ cup flour
  Pinch of salt
2 tablespoons Kentucky
  bourbon
1 cup pecans, chopped
1 cup chocolate chips
1 pie shell, partially baked

Cream butter and sugar in medium bowl. Add beaten eggs, flour, salt, and bourbon. Mix well. Fold in pecans and chocolate chips until well combined. Pour into a partially baked pie shell and bake for 30 minutes or until pie is a light, golden brown. Let cool 10 minutes. Serve warm and à la mode if desired. Enjoy!

Number of Servings: 8

About Wolf Trap Education:

Wolf Trap Institute for Early Learning Through the Arts was started with a grant from the U.S. Department of Health and Human Services, Head Start Bureau.

Perfect Pecan Pie

The ultimate recipe for this decadent dessert.

½ cup sugar
3 eggs
½ cup dark corn syrup
½ cup light corn syrup
1½ teaspoons salt
¼ cup melted butter or margarine
1½ cups pecans
1 teaspoon vanilla extract
1 unbaked pie shell

Mix sugar, eggs, and syrups together. Add salt, melted butter, pecans, and vanilla. Pour into the unbaked pie shell. Bake for 1 hour at 350 degrees.

Note:
Cover crust with foil if it begins to turn too brown while baking.

Number of Servings: 8

About Wolf Trap Education:

In 1983, Head Start asked Wolf Trap to replicate the Institute's programs outside Washington D.C. Today, regional programs exist in inner-cities, suburbs, and remote rural areas all over the country.

The Easiest and Most Delicious Chocolate Chip Cake

This should be shared and enjoyed by all!

1 package yellow cake mix
4 eggs
1 cup vegetable oil
1 cup milk
1 (3.4 ounce) box instant vanilla pudding
4 ounce bar sweet chocolate, grated
½ bag chocolate chips
Powdered sugar

Mix first six ingredients (through sweet chocolate). Fold in chocolate chips. Pour into a greased bundt pan. Bake at 350 degrees for 50-60 minutes. Remove from pan when cool.

Sprinkle with powdered sugar before serving.

Number of Servings: 8-10

About Wolf Trap Education:

The impact of the Wolf Trap Institute is felt around the world; international residencies and exchanges have taken place in England, Scotland, Wales, Northern Ireland, Ireland, Greece, Brazil, Jamaica, Canada, Italy, and Mexico.

Spoon Bread

Former First Lady Mrs. Lyndon B. Johnson

Spoon bread was one of Lyndon's mother's delightful dishes. With a salad (fruit or green) and meat, it makes a perfect lunch.

1 scant cup of corn meal
3 cups of whole milk
3 eggs
1 level teaspoon salt
3 level teaspoons baking powder
Butter the size of a walnut, melted

Lightly grease an 8x8 pan. Stir corn meal into 2 cups of milk and let mixture come to a boil, making a mush. Add the remaining milk and well-beaten eggs. Stir in salt, baking powder, and melted butter. Spread into prepared pan. Bake 30 minutes at 350 degrees.

Number of Servings: 8

About Wolf Trap Education:

In 2003, Wolf Trap Institute Teaching Artists were invited by the Greek Ministries of Culture and Education to conduct training sessions for every kindergarten teacher in Athens.

Sommelier's Best Recipe

Gray Ghost Miniature Cheesecakes

Gray Ghost Winery
14706 Lee Highway
Amissville, VA 20106

Miniature cheesecakes are a perfect finale to a lovely meal paired with Gray Ghost Adieu – a late harvest vidal dessert wine.

1 box vanilla wafers, crushed
4 eggs
4 (8 ounce) packages cream cheese
1 cup sugar
1 teaspoon vanilla extract
1 box (100) mini-size baking cups

Put 1 teaspoon vanilla wafer crumbs in each mini-size baking cup.

Beat eggs in a large bowl. Add cream cheese, sugar, and vanilla and beat until fluffy.

Put about 1 tablespoon batter into each cup. Bake 12 minutes at 350 degrees.

Number of Servings: 70

About Wolf Trap Education:

In 2003, Wolf Trap Institute for Early Learning Through the Arts reached more than 100 communities worldwide through classroom residencies, workshops for teachers and families, and field trip performances.

Juliana's Coffee Cake

Perfect for a Sunday brunch or early morning meeting.

1/4 **pound (1 stick) butter or margarine, softened**
1 1/2 **cups sugar, divided**
2 **large eggs**
8 **ounces sour cream**
3 **teaspoons baking powder**
1 **teaspoon baking soda**
1 1/2 **cups all-purpose flour**
2 **teaspoons vanilla**
2 **teaspoons cinnamon**
1/2 **cup pecans, chopped (optional)**

Preheat oven to 350 degrees. Lightly grease an 8x8 inch pan. In a large bowl, cream the butter with 1 cup of sugar; add the eggs one at a time, mixing constantly. Add the sour cream, baking powder, baking soda, flour, and vanilla.

In a separate bowl, combine the remaining 1/2 cup of sugar, cinnamon, and pecans (optional). Pour half the batter into the pan and sprinkle with 2/3 of the cinnamon sugar mixture. Pour the remaining batter on top, then sprinkle with the remaining cinnamon sugar mixture.

Bake for 40-45 minutes.

Number of Servings: 9

About Wolf Trap Education:

"As an educator in the early childhood community, I have been amazed by Wolf Trap's ability to stay one step ahead in arts-based learning. They not only understand the importance of active learning–they redefine it and teach us what it means."
–Sharon Glynn, *Director of Training, Fairfax County, Virginia, Office for Children*

Sunrise Muffins

Start your day with a delicious treat!

2½ cups all-purpose flour
1 cup packed brown sugar
2 teaspoons baking soda
2 teaspoons ground cinnamon
½ teaspoon salt
2 cups carrot, shredded
1 cup Rome or hard golden apple, shredded
¾ cup raisins
⅓ cup pecans, chopped
¼ cup flaked sweetened coconut
1 (8 ounce) can crushed pineapple in juice, drained
⅓ cup vegetable oil
⅓ cup apple butter
2 teaspoons vanilla extract
2 large eggs
2 large egg whites
Cooking spray

Preheat oven to 350 degrees.

Lightly spoon flour into dry measuring cups; level with a knife. Combine flour, and next 4 ingredients (flour through salt) in a large bowl. Stir in carrot and next 5 ingredients (carrot through pineapple); make a well in the center of mixture.

Combine oil and next 4 ingredients (oil through egg whites); stir with a whisk. Add oil mixture to flour mixture, stirring just until moist.

Spoon the batter into 24 muffin cups coated with cooking spray. Bake at 350 degrees for 25 minutes or until muffins spring back when touched lightly in center. Remove muffins from pans immediately; cool on a wire rack.

Note:
Muffins can be stored in an airtight container and frozen for up to 1 month. Wrap in foil and reheat at 300 degrees.

Number of Servings: 24

Banana Bread

It is wonderful served warm.

½ cup vegetable oil
1 cup sugar
1 egg
3 ripe bananas
1 teaspoon vanilla
1½ cups flour
1 teaspoon baking soda
1 cup pecans or walnuts, chopped
1 cup wheat germ

In a mixer combine vegetable oil and sugar until blended. Add egg and mix well. Blend in 3 ripe bananas and vanilla. Mix flour and baking soda together. Slowly add to banana mixture. Stir in chopped nuts and wheat germ.

Divide mixture in half. Bake in two loaf pans at 350 degrees for 40 minutes or until toothpick comes out clean when inserted in the middle.

Number of Servings: 8-10

About Wolf Trap Education:

Wolf Trap internships for college students across the country and around the world in the areas of arts administration, education, and technical theater offer the practical opportunity to become an integral member of the staff and to work side by side with professionals producing, promoting, and administering the full spectrum of the performing arts.

Innovative DESIGN *can add* FORM *and* FUNCTION *to your kitchen.*

A well-designed kitchen can be comfortable, inviting and responsive to every need of the family that uses it. It just requires some smart product choices and innovative design techniques, especially when it comes to countertops.

To help you create a kitchen that's tailored to the way you live, following are some tips from Reico Kitchen & Bath, the leading supplier of kitchen and bath products and services in the Washington, D.C. area.

COUNTERTOP FORM AND FUNCTION:

With hundreds of options for countertops and kitchen surfaces, it's best to narrow the scope by deciding which countertop surface best fits your needs and wishes. It is important to have the necessary information to make an informed decision about your countertop.

- Solid surface - Smooth surface that's stain- and heat-resistant. Difficult to scratch and easy to repair.

- Granite - High style with "cool" surface for handling dough. Smooth surface does not scratch easily. Durable surface with absorption and heat-resistant qualities.

- Engineered stone - Quartz surface with more color options than natural stone. Extremely durable, heat- and stain-resistant and doesn't break like stone.

- Stainless steel - Trendy professional look. Offers a cool surface that does not chip or crack.

- Laminate - Economical and available in a host of colors and patterns. Durable, easy to maintain and can be used in many settings—kitchens, baths, kids' rooms and laundry rooms.

More Function and Innovation tips from Reico can be found throughout the book.

Mother's Pickles

These are easy, crisp, and perfect with everything from pâté to egg salad to hamburgers.

8 medium pickling
    cucumbers
4 cups sugar
1 tablespoon pickling
    spices
2½ teaspoons salt
2 cups vinegar

Day 1: Place washed, unpeeled whole cucumbers in large bowl. Cover with boiling water, let stand. Do not cover; do not refrigerate.

Day 2: Drain and repeat. (Rinse cucumbers well if waxy.)

Days 3-4: Drain and repeat.

Day 5: Drain. Wash cucumbers well, then slice and place in glass oven proof bowl. Combine sugar, pickling spice, salt, and vinegar, and bring to a boil. Pour over cucumber slices. When cool, cover with plastic wrap. Do not refrigerate.

Day 6: Do nothing.

Day 7: Drain brine into pan and bring to a boil. Pour back over cucumber slices. When cool, place in refrigerator dish and cover. Refrigerate.

Pickles may be sealed, but keep for months in the refrigerator in an airtight container.

Number of Servings: 15-25

About The Barns at Wolf Trap:

USA Today called The Barns "One of 10 great places to see cabaret... the setting, in two 18th-century barns...on rolling countryside in Northern Virginia, is one of a kind." (December 28, 2001)

Favorite Vinaigrette

This is a great crowd pleaser. Double the amount so there is extra to save for another day.

¼ cup balsamic vinegar
1½ teaspoons sugar
1 tablespoon whole grain Dijon mustard with seeds
Salt and pepper to taste
1 cup extra virgin olive oil

Pour balsamic vinegar into a small mixing bowl. Whisk in the sugar, then mustard, then salt and pepper. Whisk in the olive oil until all ingredients are well blended.

Toss over any salad. Especially good over a Greek salad with tomatoes and feta cheese.

Do not refrigerate.

Number of Servings: 8-12

About The Barns at Wolf Trap:
The first performing season at The Barns in 1981 featured evenings of Baroque music, Gilbert and Sullivan music, The No Elephant Circus, and Trapezoid.

Harvest Brew

A warm spiced cider, great for book club meetings and chilly days!

$^1/_2$ teaspoon whole
    allspice
$^1/_2$ teaspoon whole cloves
1 stick cinnamon
$^1/_2$ cup water
$1^1/_2$ cups cranberry juice
    cocktail
1 quart apple cider

Combine all ingredients in a 2 quart glass casserole dish. Microwave on high 5-8 minutes until hot. Strain to remove spices. Can also be made over the stove or in a slow cooker.

Number of Servings: 12 $^1/_2$-cup servings

About The Barns at Wolf Trap:

Wolf Trap's award-winning Folk Masters series was recorded for national broadcast and for sale on CD in partnership with the Smithsonian Institution and WETA-FM. This series featured traditional artists from the Americas and the world.

Photo courtesy of Smithsonian Institution.

Marvelous Margaritas

Marvelous, golden, and perfect for any festive occasion.

⅓ cup triple sec
⅔ cup gold tequila
1 (6 ounce) can frozen lime juice
½ cup water (from lime juice can)
½ fresh lime squeezed into mixture
3-4 cups crushed ice
1 ounce orange liqueur
½ fresh lime for rim of glass
Kosher salt for rim of glass

Combine all ingredients except salt in a blender. Blend just until combined.

Take the other half of a fresh lime and coat the rim of the glass then dip it in the salt. Pour into a margarita glass.

Relax and enjoy. "It's five o'clock somewhere!"

Number of Servings: 6-8

About The Barns at Wolf Trap:

Many artists have recorded live albums at The Barns because of the venue's superb acoustics.

Miso-Ginger Vinaigrette Veggie Dressing

Everyone loves to eat their veggies at Asian restaurants because they know how to prepare them.

3-4 tablespoons miso
3-4 tablespoons fresh ginger
    root, grated
$1/4$ cup rice wine vinegar
 4 tablespoons sesame oil
$1/2$ cup olive oil
$1/2$ cup peanut oil
$1/2$ cup water
    Dash of lemon juice

Use a food processor on low speed. Start with miso, ginger, vinegar, and sesame oil. Once they are blended, stream in the olive and peanut oils slowly and steadily. Slowly stream (or trickle) in the water until it has the texture you like. With enough water, it gets more like a creamy dressing.

Toss the vinaigrette with lightly steamed or sautéed vegetables—snow peas, carrots, peppers, broccoli, bean sprouts etc., just like they do at the Asian restaurants.

Number of Servings: 2-3 cups

About The Barns at Wolf Trap:

Roomful of Blues, John McCutcheon,
The Nighthawks, Fighting Gravity, and BeauSoleil
have all recorded complete albums at The Barns.

169

Fresh Strawberry Daiquiris

2 pints fresh strawberries,
    washed and hulled
12 ounces light rum
    Juice of two fresh limes
6 tablespoons sugar syrup
    or honey
1 cup crushed ice

Mix half of all the ingredients in a blender; then repeat the process. Pour the mixture into two prechilled thermoses.

Number of Servings: 2 quarts

About The Barns at Wolf Trap:

Many master chamber music artists are featured each season at The Barns as part of *The Discovery Series*, which is recorded for national broadcast as *Center Stage from Wolf Trap*.

Sun-Dried Tomato Brandy Cream Sauce for Pasta

Natalie MacMaster - Celtic Fiddle Performer

This is an awesome sauce to put on your favorite pasta!

2 cups heavy cream
1 cup brandy
$^1/_2$ cup chopped, sun-dried tomatoes packed in oil
$^1/_4$ teaspoon salt
$^1/_4$ teaspoon black pepper

Mix all ingredients together in a deep saucepan or pot. Bring mixture to a boil on a medium heat, reduce heat and continue to simmer on low heat until mixture reduces by half and turns a caramel color. Stir mixture with a slotted spoon every 5-10 minutes (about 30 minutes).

Serve over your favorite pasta, or with chicken or shrimp.

Note:
The first time I made this I almost burned the house down! Make sure the mixture does not boil over as the brandy will catch fire. Cook in a very deep pot.

Number of Servings: 6-8

Summer Delight White Sangria

Ripe melon and citrus flavors.

½ cup granulated sugar
½ cup orange liqueur
½ cup brandy
2 bottles dry white wine
  (750 ml. each)
1 quart club soda, chilled
  Honeydew melon and
  cantaloupe balls
  Lemon, lime, and
  orange slices
  Whole strawberries
  Ice cubes

In a large pitcher, combine the sugar, orange liqueur, brandy, and wine; cover and refrigerate for 1-2 hours until chilled. Just before serving, stir in club soda to taste; add melon balls, lemon, lime, and orange slices, strawberries, and ice cubes.

For classic sangria:
Combine 1 bottle (750 ml.) of dry red wine with 6 orange slices, 6 lemon slices, 2 tablespoons each orange liqueur and brandy, and 1 tablespoon granulated sugar. Cover and refrigerate for 1 hour. Just before serving, add 1 quart club soda and lots of ice cubes. Taste and add sugar or soda as desired.

Number of Servings: 12

Spiced Nuts

A wonderful and tasty treat.

1 cup sugar
1/2 teaspoon salt
1 teaspoon cinnamon
1/4 teaspoon cayenne
1/4 teaspoon ground
   cloves
1/4 teaspoon nutmeg
2 tablespoons butter
1 teaspoon vanilla extract
2 tablespoons water
1 cup pecans, or any
   mixture of pecans,
   cashews, and walnuts,
   toasted

Combine sugar, salt, cinnamon, cayenne, cloves, nutmeg, butter, vanilla, and water in a large saucepan. Stirring constantly, cook until soft ball stage (when a small amount dropped into cold water forms a soft ball). Stir in the toasted nuts.

Remove from the heat and stir until no longer glossy. Pour onto a buttered baking sheet and spread. Cool and break into pieces.

Number of Servings: 8-10

About The Barns at Wolf Trap:

Famous performers who played at The Barns before they were household names include Mary Chapin Carpenter, Lyle Lovett, John Hiatt, Alison Krauss, Patty Loveless, Faith Hill, Branford Marsalis, Vince Gill, Harry Connick, Jr., and Jeff Daniels.

Sparkling Strawberry Mint Lemonade

Light and refreshing.

1 pint water
6 ounces fresh mint sprigs
  or 2 ounces dried
  peppermint
4 ounces sugar
$\frac{1}{2}$ pint lemon juice
$1\frac{1}{4}$ pounds strawberries,
  hulled
  **Dry sparkling wine or
  sparkling water**

In a pan, bring the water and mint to a boil. Cover and simmer for 5 minutes, stirring occasionally. Strain (through cheesecloth if using the dried herb), discarding mint, and return liquid to the pan. Stir in the sugar. Reduce liquid to $\frac{1}{2}$ pint. Stir in the lemon juice.

If desired, reserve about a quarter of the strawberries as a garnish and slice them thinly. Purée the remaining strawberries with some of the syrup mixture in a blender. Pour into a large pitcher. Taste and add more sugar if needed. Stir in sliced berries and remaining syrup and chill.

To serve:
Stir fruit mixture, then pour about 4 tablespoons into a small glass, fill with sparkling wine or water and stir.

Number of Servings: 6-8

Fireside Mulled Wine

1 lemon
2 cups water
⅔ cup sugar
1 teaspoon whole cloves
½ teaspoon allspice
2 cinnamon sticks
1 bottle Burgundy wine
¼ cup brandy

Slice the lemon crosswise and combine with water, sugar, and spices. Simmer gently for 10 minutes. Reduce the heat and add wine and the brandy. Heat until very hot, but not boiling. Serve with cinnamon sticks.

Number of Servings: yields 1 quart

About The Barns at Wolf Trap:

Come inside The Barns and you will immediately feel its rustic charm. The larger German barn, where the performances take place, was built in the early part of the 18th-century. The medium-sized Scottish barn, which now serves as a bar and reception area, was built in 1790s.

Exotic Fruit Smoothie

½ cup chopped ice
½ cup papaya nectar
1 banana, cut into 1 inch pieces
1 cup fresh pineapple chunks
¼ cup raspberries
4 slices starfruit (optional)

In a blender, combine the ice, papaya nectar, banana, pineapple, and raspberries, and blend until smooth. Pour into glasses and garnish with starfruit, if desired.

Number of Servings: 4

Aioli

Aioli is a garlic and oil condiment used throughout the Mediterranean region in soups, stews, and seafood preparations.

2 extra large egg yolks,
  room temperature
6 cloves garlic, mashed to
  a paste with coarse salt
¼ cup olive oil
¼ cup extra virgin olive oil
1 teaspoon lemon juice
¼ teaspoon kosher salt
¼ teaspoon white pepper

Aioli is best made in a mortar crushing the garlic with a pestle and constantly working in the oils. For those without this equipment, a mini processor will do. In the bowl of a food processor, place the egg yolks and mashed garlic paste. With the processor running very slowly add the oils in a stream until all is incorporated. Add the lemon juice, salt, and pepper. If too thick, add in a little water.

About The Barns at Wolf Trap:

Wolf Trap produced its own live CD at The Barns entitled *Raise the Roof: A Retrospective Live from The Barns at Wolf Trap* in Fall 2004. This album features tracks from various artists including Tom Paxton, Chris Smither, Nils Lofgren, The Grandsons, and The Iguanas.

Minty Mint Juleps

Perfect for a day at the races.

1 cup water
2¼ cups sugar
½ cup fresh mint leaves, packed
2 cups bourbon
Crushed ice
Mint sprigs

Make syrup the day before. Boil water with sugar for 5 minutes. Cool. Add packed mint leaves and allow to steep 12 hours or overnight, stirring occasionally. Strain syrup through cheesecloth and discard the mint.

Combine the bourbon with the minted syrup. Chill until needed. Mixture should be very cold. Fill julep cup or tumbler with crushed ice. Pour the chilled minted bourbon into each cup. Insert a mint sprig into the ice so that the leaves graze the rim. Put a short straw at the opposite side of the glass.

Hint:
When you drink mint juleps, your nose should be close enough to the cup to smell the mint leaves.

Number of Servings: 6-8

About The Barns at Wolf Trap:

The idea of reassembling a historic barn on this site came directly from Wolf Trap founder, Catherine Filene Shouse. She felt that the excellent acoustical qualities of such a building would provide an ideal place to experience live performances and hired renowned barn historian Richard Babcock to find the buildings.

Mango and Yogurt Smoothie

A cool and refreshing treat for warm summer evenings.

2 mangos (about
    2¼ pounds total)
½ cup plain yogurt
½ cup crushed ice
1½ cups orange juice

Peel and seed the mangos and cut into chunks. In a blender or food processor, purée the mangos, yogurt, and ice. Blend in orange juice. Place in a thermos and shake before serving

To serve:
Pour into stemmed glasses.

Hint:
This recipe is also delicious made with 3 cups of cubed cantaloupe.

Number of Servings: 4

About The Barns at Wolf Trap:

The Barns were moved piece by piece from their original locations in upstate New York. Both barns were carefully measured, photographed, and sketched before they were painstakingly dismantled. Each barn was brought to Babcock's workshop in Massachusetts to be restored before being brought to Virginia.

181

Smokehouse Barbecue Sauce

Accompanies BBQ Beef Brisket recipe on page 91.

2 (14 ounce) bottles catsup
3 tablespoons each horseradish and Dijon mustard
2 tablespoons Worcestershire sauce
1 tablespoon lemon juice
1 teaspoon celery seed
$1/4$ teaspoon each onion salt, cayenne pepper, liquid smoke, garlic juice

Blend mixture thoroughly.

Refrigerate in a glass jar.

Perfect topping for your chicken and ribs.

Number of Servings: 12-15

Hot Toddy

¼ lemon
1½ teaspoons sugar
2 whole cloves
2-3 ounces bourbon
Very hot water

Squeeze the lemon juice into a heatproof cup. Add the sugar, cloves, and bourbon. Stir until the sugar is dissolved. Add hot water.

Hint:
To make in large quantities, combine the first four ingredients in desired quantity.

Number of Servings: 1

About The Barns at Wolf Trap:
The Barns were reconstructed using the 18th century building techniques of block and tackle. The crew hoisted the beams with a system of gin poles, ropes, and pulleys, much like an old-fashioned barn raising.

Appliance TRENDS *increase* FUNCTION *to your kitchen.*

Life in the kitchen can be a dream come true for food enthusiasts who say that high-performance, high-tech gear tops their wish list. Appliance manufacturers have introduced options that make food preparation and cleanup simpler, faster and more efficient.

To help you create a kitchen that's tailored to the way you live, following are some product trend tips from Reico Kitchen & Bath, the leading supplier of kitchen and bath products and services in the Washington, D.C. area.

APPLIANCES:

- Custom refrigerators offer you a refrigerator designed to suit your cooling and storage needs. You may have certain needs and wishes based on your cooking styles. All of these wishes can be taken into account to get the kitchen of your dreams.

- Multiple dishwashers are being used in the kitchen. In some cases, one dishwasher is used primarily for clean dishes and the other for dirty dishes. And to minimize bending, dishwashers also are being installed raised off the floor.

- Ovens have never offered more features. Some cook up to five times faster than conventional ovens while others offer fully-programmable, digital capabilities that automatically select the optimal cooking mode and temperature.

- Make cooking easier for you and your family by incorporating the work triangle—sink, cooking surface and refrigerator—in a centralized area.

- Position your appliances so everything is easy to access to make it efficient to work in the kitchen.

For additional tips to customize your kitchen, contact a Reico Kitchen & Bath designer. Reico's professional staff takes the time to get to know you as a customer, understand your needs and wishes and ensure the room of your dreams is delivered for a hassle-free Reico experience.

Helpful Tips

Emergency Substitutions

INGREDIENT	AMOUNT	SUBSTITUTION
Baking Powder	1 teaspoon	$\frac{1}{4}$ teaspoon baking soda plus $\frac{1}{2}$ teaspoon cream of tartar
Buttermilk	1 cup	1 cup plain yogurt or 1 tablespoon vinegar plus milk to equal 1 cup or 1 tablespoon lemon juice plus milk to equal one cup
Cake flour	1 cup	1 cup minus 2 tablespoons sifted all-purpose flour
Chocolate, unsweetened	1 ounce (1 square)	3 tablespoons unsweetened cocoa plus 1 tablespoon butter or margarine
Cornstarch	1 tablespoon	2 tablespoons all-purpose flour
Corn syrup	2 cups	1 cup granulated sugar
Cream, heavy	see Cream, whipping	
Cream, light	1 cup	$1\frac{1}{2}$ tablespoons butter plus whole milk to equal 1 cup
Cream, whipping	1 cup	$\frac{1}{2}$ cup butter plus whole milk to equal 1 cup
Egg yolk	2 yolks	1 whole egg (can be used for baking but not for a piecrust or a sauce)
Egg whole	1 egg	2 egg yolks (for baking, 2 egg yolks plus 1 tablespoon water)

Emergency Substitutions, continued

INGREDIENT	AMOUNT	SUBSTITUTION
Herbs, fresh	1 tablespoon	1 teaspoon dried herbs
Honey	1 cup	$1\frac{1}{4}$ cups granulated sugar
Lemon juice	1 tablespoon	1 tablespoon distilled white vinegar
Milk, skim	1 cup	$\frac{1}{3}$ cup nonfat dry milk plus $\frac{3}{4}$ cup water
Milk, whole	1 cup	$\frac{1}{2}$ cup evaporated milk plus $\frac{1}{2}$ cup water
Molasses	1 cup	$\frac{3}{4}$ cup granulated sugar
Mushrooms, fresh	1 pound	12 ounces canned mushrooms, drained
Mustard, dry	1 teaspoon	1 tablespoon prepared mustard
Sour cream	1 cup	3 tablespoons butter plus buttermilk or yogurt to equal 1 cup
Sugar, brown	1 cup	1 cup granulated sugar
Sugar, granulated	1 cup	$1\frac{3}{4}$ cups confectioners' sugar (Do not substitute for baking)
Tomato juice	3 cups	$1\frac{1}{2}$ cups tomato sauce plus $1\frac{1}{2}$ cups water
Tomato sauce	1 cup	1 can (3 ounce size) tomato paste plus $\frac{1}{2}$ cup water
Yogurt	1 cup	1 cup buttermilk

Food Weights and Measures

WEIGHT/MEASURE	EQUIVALENT
Dash	less than $1/8$ teaspoon
$1\frac{1}{2}$ teaspoons	$1/2$ tablespoon
3 teaspoons	1 tablespoon
2 tablespoons	$1/8$ cup (1 fluid ounce)
4 tablespoons	$1/4$ cup (2 fluid ounces)
$5\frac{1}{3}$ tablespoons	$1/3$ cup (5 tablespoons plus 1 teaspoon)
8 tablespoons	$1/2$ cup (4 fluid ounces)
$10\frac{2}{3}$ tablespoons	$2/3$ cup (10 tablespoons plus 2 teaspoons)
12 tablespoons	$3/4$ cup (6 fluid ounces)
16 tablespoons	1 cup (8 fluid ounces)
$3/8$ cup	$1/4$ cup plus 2 tablespoons
$5/8$ cup	$1/2$ cup plus 2 tablespoons
$7/8$ cup	$3/4$ cup plus 2 tablespoons
1 tablespoon	$1/2$ fluid ounce
1 cup	$1/2$ pint (8 fluid ounces)
2 cups	1 pint (16 fluid ounces)
4 cups	1 quart (32 fluid ounces)
2 pints	1 quart

Weights and Measures, continued

WEIGHT/MEASURE	EQUIVALENT
2 quarts	$\frac{1}{2}$ gallon
4 quarts (liquid)	1 gallon
8 quarts (dry)	1 peck
4 pecks	1 bushel
16 ounces (dry)	1 pound
1 gram	.035 ounces
1 kilogram	2.21 pounds
1 ounce	28.35 grams
1 teaspoon	4.9 milliliters
1 tablespoon	14.8 milliliters
1 cup	236.6 milliliters
1 liter	1.06 quarts or 1000 milliliters

Ingredient Equivalents

INGREDIENT	EQUIVALENT
CHOCOLATE	
1 cup semi-sweet chocolate pieces	6-ounce package semi-sweet chocolate pieces
1 ounce unsweetened chocolate	1 square unsweetened chocolate
CRUMBS	
1 cup bread cubes	2 slices bread
1 cup soft bread crumbs	1$\frac{1}{2}$ to 2 slices bread
1 cup dry bread crumbs	4 slices bread
1 cup graham cracker crumbs	14 graham cracker squares
1 cup finely crushed vanilla wafer crumbs	22 vanilla wafers
1 cup chocolate wafer crumbs	19 chocolate wafers
1 cup finely crushed gingersnap crumbs	15 gingersnaps
DAIRY	
$\frac{1}{2}$ cup butter or margarine	1 stick ($\frac{1}{4}$ pound) butter or margarine
6 tablespoons cream cheese	3-ounce package cream cheese
1 cup cream cheese	8-ounce package cream cheese
1 cup crumbled blue cheese	4 ounces crumbled blue cheese
1$\frac{1}{4}$ cups grated cheese	$\frac{1}{4}$ pound hard cheese (Parmesan, Romano)

Ingredient Equivalents, continued

INGREDIENT	EQUIVALENT
DAIRY (continued)	
1 cup shredded hard cheese (Cheddar, Swiss)	4 ounces hard cheese
1$\frac{1}{4}$ cups shredded soft cheese (American, Monterey Jack)	4 ounces soft cheese
2 cups whipped cream	1 cup heavy cream or 1 cup whipping cream
FRUIT	
1 cup sliced apple	1 large apple
1$\frac{1}{2}$ cups mashed banana	3 medium bananas
2 cups sliced banana	3 medium bananas
2 to 3 tablespoons freshly squeezed lemon juice	1 medium lemon
2 teaspoons grated lemon zest	1 medium lemon
1$\frac{1}{2}$ to 2 tablespoons freshly squeezed lime juice	1 medium lime
1$\frac{1}{2}$ teaspoons grated lime zest	1 medium lime
1$\frac{3}{4}$ to 2 cups berries	1 pint berries
3$\frac{1}{2}$ to 4 cups berries	1 quart berries
NUTS	
1-1$\frac{1}{4}$ cups almond nutmeats	1 pound almonds in shells
3 to 3$\frac{1}{2}$ cups chopped almonds	1 pound almonds, shelled

Ingredient Equivalents, continued

INGREDIENT	EQUIVALENT

NUTS (continued)

INGREDIENT	EQUIVALENT
2 to 2½ cups pecan nutmeats	1 pound pecans in shells
4 cups chopped pecans	1 pound pecans, shelled
1½ to 2 cups walnut meats	1 pound walnuts in shells
4 cups chopped walnuts	1 pound walnuts, shelled

PASTA, RICE

2 to 2½ cups cooked pasta (depending on shape)	¼ pound dried (uncooked) pasta
3 cups cooked rice	1 cup raw long grain white rice

SUGAR

2 cups granulated sugar	1 pound box granulated sugar
2¼ cups brown sugar, firmly packed	1 pound box brown sugar
4 cups confectioners' sugar, sifted	1 pound box confectioners' sugar

VEGETABLES

4½ cups shredded cabbage	1 small head cabbage (1 pound)
1 cup grated carrot	1 large carrot
1 cup diced or chopped celery	2 medium celery stalks
1 cup diced green pepper	1 large green pepper
6 cups torn lettuce	1 medium head of lettuce

Ingredient Equivalents, continued

INGREDIENT	EQUIVALENT
3 cups sliced raw mushrooms	$3/4$ pound raw mushrooms
$1/2$ cup chopped onion	1 medium onion
$1^3/4$ cups mashed potato	3 medium potatoes

MISCELLANEOUS

$1/2$ cup crumbled bacon	8 slices of bacon
1 cup dried beans or peas	$1/2$ pound dried beans or peas
$2^1/4$ to $2^1/2$ cups cooked beans or peas	1 cup dried beans or peas
1 cup beef or chicken broth	1 bouillon cube or 1 envelope bouillon dissolved in 1 cup boiling water
2 cups cooked chicken	1 large boned whole chicken breast
3 cups cooked chicken	$3^1/2$ pounds raw whole chicken
1 tablespoon chopped fresh herbs	1 teaspoon dried herbs
$1/2$ pound shelled and deveined cooked shrimp	1 pound raw shrimp in shell shrimp

Acknowledgements

Special thanks to

REICO KITCHEN AND BATH
Major Sponsor

Cookbook Supporters

Chef's Best
Indebleu Restaurant - Vikram Garg
Melrose Restaurant - Brian McBride

Sommelier
Gray Ghost Vineyards -
    Cheryl G. Kellert
Oasis Winery -
    Mr. and Mrs. Tareq D. Salahi

Grand Chef
Robin Crawford Heller
Ann M. McKee
Stella Guerra Nelson

Master Chef
Stanley E. Collender
Barbara Friedman
Virginia McGehee Friend
April Georgelas
Carol Ann Hayashida
John and Tracy Jacquemin
Barbara A. Kampf
Suzann Wilson Matthews
Juliana and Richard E. May
Darrell L. Netherton

Hon. Norine E. Noonan, Ph.D.
Mollie and John Ottina
Eloise C. Poretz
Elizabeth Reinhardt
Tina Small

Executive Chef
Jean AbiNader
Marilynn D. Bersoff
Nancy B. Carlson
Lilyan Chitlik
Tiffany and Tom Conaway
Ellen K. Fishbein
Ruth Gresser - Pizzeria Paradiso
    Restaurant
Anne Gutman
Diane B. Kirik
Gary and Kelly Nakamoto
Bonnie Rountree
Bill and Vicky Sabo
Elizabeth A. Scully and Daniel J. Lynn
Lynn Doe Shipway
John and Nina Toups
Liv Syvrud Violette
Ruthanna Weber

195

Sous Chef

Dr. and Mrs. William Binder
Phyllis Orenstein Bresler
Roxy Chitlik
Cissel Goff Collins
Margaret R. Fitch
Barbara C. Flynn
Margaret A. Fromme
Ellen G. Goodman
Monica A. Malouf
Sophia Z. Myers
Harriet Pilger
Susan Poretz
Stacey Reynolds
Madelyn and Bill Stephens
Marjorie W. Vanderbilt
Sarah Currie Walters
Faye Wickersham

Recipe Contributors

Bill Banks
Marilynn D. Bersoff
Phyllis Orenstein Bresler
Jeffery Buben - Vidalia Restaurant
Nancy B. Carlson
Marcia Myers Carlucci
Valerie Carroll
Scott Chambers - La Ferme
    Restaurant
Lilyan Chitlik
Roxy Chitlik
Tiffany and Tom Conaway
Marcia Daft
Ted Davis
Frieda Fetzer
Margaret R. Fitch
Barbara C. Flynn
Barbara Friedman
Martha Dale Fritts

Rowena Fullinwider
Vikram Garg - Indebleu Restaurant
April Georgelas
Wayne Gibbens
Ellen Goodman
Gray Ghost Vineyard
Anne Gutman
Ruth Gresser - Pizzeria Paradiso
Mary Henderson
Jo Hodgin
Tracy Jacquemin
Terrence D. Jones
Susan Kadar
Barbara A. Kampt
Cheryl G. Kellert - Gray Ghost
    Vineyard
Bob Kinkead - Kinkeads Restaurant
Akua Kouyate
Carol M. Lascaris
Barbara Lewis
Monica A. Malouf
Jean Marumoto
Suzanne Wilson Matthews
Brian McBride - Melrose Restaurant
Sophia Z. Meyers
Darrell L. Netherton
Hon. Norine E. Noonan, Ph.D.
Mollie and John Ottina
Harriet M. Pilger
Eloise C. Poretz
Susan Poretz
Joe Raffa - Majestic Café
Libby Rector
Stacey Reynolds
Michel Richard - Citronelle
    Restaurant
Bonnie Rountree
Mary Kay Shelton
Lynn Doe Shipway
Tina Small
Allyson Taubman
John and Nina Toups
Fabio Trabocchi - Maestro Restaurant
Robin Boyers Underwood

196

Marjorie Vanderbilt
Liv Syvrud Violette
Sarah Currie Walters
Charlie Walters
Terry Walters
Ruthanna Weber
Donna Wegner
Faye Wickersham
Bob Wilson
Mr. and Mrs. Tareq D. Salahi -
   Oasis Winery
Peter Zimmerman

Celebrity Recipes
John Anthony
Clint Black
Mrs. Barbara Bush
Arch Campbell
Mormon Tabernacle Choir
Mrs. Rosalynn Carter
John Eaton
The Hon. and Mrs. Newt Gingrich
Goldy
John Gorka
Marvin Hamlisch
Bruce Hornsby
Rebecca Lynn Howard
Mrs. Lyndon B. Johnson
B.B. King
Keith Lockhart
Natalie MacMaster
Maureen McGovern
Kenny Rogers
Leonard Slatkin
Dick Smothers
Tom Smothers
Paul Taylor
Trisha Yearwood

Chef's Best Recipes
Vikram Garg - INDEBLEU
   Restaurant
Brian McBride - Melrose Restaurant

Sommelier's Best Recipes
Gray Ghost Vineyard
Oasis Winery

Recipe Testers

Jean AbiNader
Robert Cerbone
Angela Ciolettti
Ted Davis
Chris Faessen
Lori Fischetti
Ellen Fishbein
Fran Frazier
Georgia Grena
Carol Hayashida
Jo Hodgin
Terry Holzheimer
Elizabeth Hopkins
Ricki Kanter
Diane Kirik
Monica Malouf
Jaana Moilanen
Gary Nakamoto
Eloise Poretz
Elizabeth Reinhardt
Michelle Rounds
Jackie Rucker
Anthony Sigmon
Yoanna Talopp
Marjorie Vanderbilt
Dagnia Zeidlickis

Wolf Trap Associates Board of Directors

Ms. Lisa Collis, *First Lady of Virginia, Honorary Chairman*
Eloise C. Poretz, *Chairman*
Terry Holzheimer, *Vice Chairman*
Ellen K. Fishbein, *Secretary*

Mr. Jean R. AbiNader
Mr. Danny Aranza
Ms. Nanci E. Banks
Mr. Eric A. Campbell
Mr. Robert A. Cerbone
Ms. Carol A. Hayashida
Ms. Elizabeth Hopkins
Ms. Ricki Kanter
Ms. Diane Kirik
Mr. Mark C. Lowham

Ms. Monica A. Malouf
Ms. Juliana E. May
Mr. Brian F.X. Murphy
Mr. Gary G. Nakamoto
Mr. Darrell L. Netherton
Mrs. Christie Hart Newton
Mr. Michael James Rebibo
Ms. Elizabeth Reinhardt
Mr. Donald Richardson
Ms. Elizabeth A. Scully

Ms. Marjorie W. Vanderbilt
Mrs. Margie Wheedleton
Ms. Dagnia Zeidlickis

Ms. Lori Fischetti,
    Senior Director,
    Wolf Trap Foundation
    Events and Associates

As of January 12, 2005

Index

(Alphabetical by chapter)

Appetizers, Salads & Soups

Desserts & Breads

Beverages and Sauces